THE AMAZING DR. CLITTERHOUSE

THE AMAZING

DR. CLITTERHOUSE

A PLAY IN THREE ACTS BY

BARRÉ LYNDON

RANDOM HOUSE · NEW YORK

COPYRIGHT, 1937, BY
BARRÉ LYNDON

THE AMAZING DR. CLITTERHOUSE

Produced by Gilbert Miller at the Hudson Theatre, New York City, March 2, 1937, with the following cast:

(In the Order of Their Appearance)

NURSE ANN	Helen Trenholme
DR. CLITTERHOUSE, M.R.C.P.	Cedric Hardwicke
CHIEF-INSPECTOR CHARLES	Edward Fielding
BENNY KELLERMAN	Clarence Derwent
"PAL" GREEN	Ernest Jay
DAISY	Muriel Hutchison
SERGEANT BATES	Stephen Fox
A CONSTABLE	Ralph Sumpter
"OAKIE"	Alexander Field
"TUG" WILSON	Ross Chetwynd
"BADGER" LEE	Victor R. Beecroft
SIR WILLIAM GRANT, K.C.	Frederic Worlock

Staged by LEWIS ALLEN
Settings by RAYMOND SOVEY

SCENES

ACT I

ACT II

ACT III

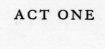

ACT ONE

ACT ONE

Scene I

Scene: dr. clitterhouse's *consulting room, at one o'clock in the morning.*

nurse ann *is reading a book by the fire. She is in love with* dr. clitterhouse, *but he has no idea of this.*

"Westminster" music is heard before the play begins. As the curtain rises a clock strikes "four quarters" then one o'clock. ann *looks toward window, then at clock on mantelpiece. As her head goes back to her book, the noise of a car is heard off stage.* ann *rises, goes to window. Light from headlamps swings into room.* ann *puts book on table above fireplace, goes to coffee table. She plugs in percolator, crosses to fireplace. The headlamp light goes out.* ann *turns chair round with a thud, giving* clitterhouse *his cue to enter.*

CLITTERHOUSE
(Enters from garden, carrying his bag)
Oh, hello, Nurse! ... Waiting up for me? *(Closes curtains.)*

ANN
Not exactly, Doctor. Only ... I wondered what had happened to you.

CLITTERHOUSE
(Going to couch)
Why?

ANN
Nurse Harvey has telephoned—twice.

3

CLITTERHOUSE

Oh ... (*Puts bag on couch.* ANN *switches on the room lights.*)

ANN

I understood you were calling there....

CLITTERHOUSE

(*At couch. Hat and coat off. Hat on head of couch. Coat on foot*)
I was held up ... How's the patient?

ANN

Not sleeping.

CLITTERHOUSE

(*Takes blood pressure apparatus from ledge of cupboard*)
That won't do ... in his weak state. Try and get Nurse Harvey for me. (ANN *crosses to desk. She begins to dial a number*) I expect she's worried. (*He takes apparatus and drops to behind coffee table*) I say ... coffee?

ANN

Yes ... I thought you might like some. It's been ready for over an hour.

CLITTERHOUSE

Have you been waiting that long? You should have gone home to bed.

ANN

I was a little bothered about Nurse Harvey's patient ... I didn't know where you were.

CLITTERHOUSE

I was all right. (*Takes jacket off and puts it over back of chair.*)

4

ANN
(*Smiling*)

But still it's one o'clock in the morning, Doctor. Are you going to do a blood pressure?

CLITTERHOUSE

I am.

ANN

Not your own.

CLITTERHOUSE

Yes.

ANN

Nothing wrong, I hope?

CLITTERHOUSE

Do I look as if there were? (*Rolls up sleeve.*)

ANN

You look rather tired.

CLITTERHOUSE
(*Eagerly*)

Do I? Noticeably?

ANN

Well, your eyes—(*Into phone*) Hello! Is that Nurse Harvey? Doctor Clitterhouse here. One moment, please. (*Holds receiver across desk to his ear.*)

CLITTERHOUSE
(*Rolling up other sleeve*)

Hello, Nurse. I'm sorry, but I was delayed. Restless, eh?

5

Well you have some paraldehyde there, I believe.... One drachm, Nurse. That's right. (ANN *takes back receiver.*)

ANN

Yes... yes. Just a moment. (*Covers mouthpiece and speaks to* CLITTERHOUSE) She seems worried.

CLITTERHOUSE
(ANN *goes behind him to end of desk*)
Give it to me. (*Into phone*) Hello. Yes... Yes... We shan't lose the old buffer. Nurse, listen to me. He's been through a lot and his nerves are all to pieces. Give him the paraldehyde and sit with him till he dozes off. Look here, would you like me to come over? You're sure? All right then, first thing in the morning. Good night... and don't worry. He may be seventy-six but he's tough... (*Replaces receiver*) Now then. (ANN *winds bandage above his elbow*) He hasn't got good eyesight, has he?

ANN

Nurse Harvey's patient? No.

CLITTERHOUSE

Does he go to bed in his spectacles?

ANN

In his spectacles? ... Why?

CLITTERHOUSE

Because Nurse Harvey's a thundering fine nurse, and you can tell her I said so. But when she's worried, she's got a face like a sick horse. Ready? (*Bandage on, she closes valve.*)

6

ANN

What *is* this for, Doctor?

CLITTERHOUSE

When taking the pressure of a nervous patient, the operator should adopt a cool and soothing manner ... Now—(*Looking at gauge*) you pump up. (ANN *works bulb.* BOTH *watch indicator. He takes own pulse at same time.*)

ANN

There's nothing to worry about there! (*Hands him bulb and goes to percolator. Removes plug and starts to pour.*)

CLITTERHOUSE
(*Rather disappointed*)

There isn't, is there? It *was* up before I went out though ... I thought it might be still ... (*Takes bandage off*) Oh, well. (*Rolls sleeve down. Goes to jacket over back of chair. Takes notebook from his jacket pocket. Returns to desk, looks at his watch and makes a note.*)

ANN
(*Crosses with coffee*)

Was that an experiment of some sort?

CLITTERHOUSE
(*Standing near desk*)

I suppose one might call it that. Thanks! Where's your coffee? (*Still writing.*)

ANN
(*Goes back to table*)

Here. (*Picks up own cup.*)

CLITTERHOUSE

(*Looks up and sees her still standing*)
Won't you sit down? (*Does up cuff link.*)

ANN

Yes, thank you. (*Sits on arm of chair*) This is not very professional, is it? (*Drinks.*)

CLITTERHOUSE

(*Picks up cup, sits back in chair*)
Well, who wants to be professional at this time of night?
You always are, though, aren't you? (*Drinks.*)

ANN

(*Looks at him*)
Well, I have to be.... (*Drinks.*)

CLITTERHOUSE

Tell me, Nurse, are you ever really—human?

ANN

Yes ... quite. Sometimes.

CLITTERHOUSE

All right, I only wanted to know. (*Drinks*) Good coffee,
that! (*Puts cup down. Then takes book from top drawer.*)

ANN

I'm glad you like it. (*Rises, goes to coffee table and puts cup
down*) You're not going to do anything more tonight, are you,
Doctor?

8

CLITTERHOUSE

(Unlocking book)

There are some notes I must finish.

ANN

It's very late, and you have a first call on Mrs. Sunning's little boy.

CLITTERHOUSE

(Rises, goes to chair and puts on jacket)

Yes ... that young rascal ... How is he?

ANN

(At coffee table)

I telephoned at ten o'clock. He was very comfortable. *(Takes jug to fireplace)* ... Cuddling that little woolly dog you gave him.

CLITTERHOUSE

Woolly dog! Yes. That caught his fancy—but it won't stop him hitting me on the nose in the morning ... *(Goes to desk.)*

ANN

It will be nice to see him running round again. *(Crosses to fireplace with milk jug.)*

CLITTERHOUSE

Grand! I like kids. They make good patients. They don't worry.

ANN

(Goes to couch for his coat)

Some are darlings. Well, if you don't want me any more, I think I ought to be getting home to bed.

9

CLITTERHOUSE

All right, Nurse. Thank you so much. Good night. (*Opening book.*)

ANN
(*Picking up his coat, goes to door*)
Good night, Doctor. (*Pauses*) Oh, Doctor, you've picked up some paint from somewhere.

CLITTERHOUSE
(*Startled*)
What?

ANN
Look.

CLITTERHOUSE
(*Rises. Goes quickly, takes coat*)
That was careless.... Can you get it off for me?

ANN
Now?

CLITTERHOUSE
Yes ... yes, now!

ANN
(*Going to couch*)
Yes, some ether will do.

CLITTERHOUSE

That was careless of me. (*Goes to fireplace.* CLITTERHOUSE *examines coat with back to her.* ANN *goes to bag. Takes it to desk corner and stares in amazement at its contents.*)

10

ANN

Doctor, this can't be your bag!

CLITTERHOUSE
(*Turns sharply*)
Don't touch that! (*Throws coat on chair*) Now who the devil gave you permission to open that bag?

ANN

I'm sorry.

CLITTERHOUSE
Ha! Ha! I'm sorry, Nurse ... (*Pause*) I shouldn't have spoken to you like that.

ANN

I thought the ether would be in here.

CLITTERHOUSE
Of course ... naturally.

ANN

I didn't realize ...

CLITTERHOUSE
Don't be so alarmed.... It's all over now.

ANN

They're ... beautiful, aren't they?

CLITTERHOUSE
I suppose they are ... (*Picks up pearls*) What do you think of this? (*Watching her.*)

ANN

That's lovely.

CLITTERHOUSE

Hm! ... I haven't much eye for these things, though.

ANN
(*Picks up brooch*)
And this brooch! You know, Doctor ... these ought to be kept in proper cases.

CLITTERHOUSE
(*Still watching her*)
They were in cases ... until I took them out.

ANN

I should be afraid to own such lovely things! (*Puts brooch back.*)

CLITTERHOUSE
(*Replaces pearls in bag*)
By the way, Nurse, at the moment, we're being strictly professional.

ANN

Strictly ... professional?

CLITTERHOUSE

Well, I didn't mean you to see this.... It's all very confidential.

ANN

Well, I don't ... quite understand ... but, of course, you can trust me, Doctor.

CLITTERHOUSE

That's very fortunate.... Because, you see, all this is...
stolen property.

ANN

Stolen!

CLITTERHOUSE

With these hands, Nurse. (*Holds out hands, palm down*)
Not a tremor. That's pretty good, you know.

ANN

What do you mean?

CLITTERHOUSE

Good nerves. I needed them when you opened that bag.
(*Walks away a little toward chair*) If you'll excuse what I
believe to be thieves' slang. I'm in the position of an old lag
caught with the swag....

ANN

You don't really mean that you've stolen these things?

CLITTERHOUSE

To be frank with you, they are the proceeds of my fourth
burglary.

ANN
(*Laughing*)

Why! Impossible!

CLITTERHOUSE

At Cranston Lodge.

ANN

The Ducketts' house?

CLITTERHOUSE

Yes. (*Turns to* ANN) But not one of my patients, I'd have you note. . . . I never shoot at sitters. . . . Here, this paint. (*Picks up coat from chair.*)

ANN

Oh, yes. (*She crosses to top cupboard for bottle of ether and cloth. He sits on arm of chair.*)

ANN

(*Coming toward him*)

I suppose you picked up the paint whilst you were breaking in? (*Laughing.*)

CLITTERHOUSE

I think it must have been off the sill of the kitchen window. . . . They had the damn place done up last week. (ANN *wets cloth and hands it to him, re-corking bottle. Then sits on edge of desk, facing him.*)

ANN

(*Laughing*)

So you broke in through the kitchen, did you, Doctor?

CLITTERHOUSE

Yes, and I forced the catch with a scalpel. . . . It might have been made for the job!

ANN

I hope you didn't leave any fingerprints.

14

CLITTERHOUSE

My gloves are in the bag. (ANN *looks in bag*) Now do you believe me? (*Rubs sleeve.*)

ANN

(*Seated on edge of desk*)

Of course I don't. It's absurd. Your friend Inspector Charles ought to hear you talking like this!

CLITTERHOUSE

(*Working on sleeve*)

It would surprise him, wouldn't it? As a matter of fact, I shall probably secure the attention of the whole of Scotland Yard before I've done here. This is getting it off all right. (*Holds out cloth for more ether.*)

ANN

(*Smiling. Steps to him. Pours ether on cloth*)

I suppose you have to guard against little clues like this?

CLITTERHOUSE

I left my hat behind at my third burglary and had to go back for it.

ANN

(*Again sits on edge of desk*)

Oh, where was that?

CLITTERHOUSE

Lady Challing's ...

ANN

(*Playing up to him*)

Oh, yes, last week! I read about it in the paper ...

CLITTERHOUSE

That was me ... and a very neat job I made of it too

ANN

Let me see. ... The burglars got in from the ...

CLITTERHOUSE

I got in, you mean.

ANN

Oh, yes, of course. *You* got in from the garage roof.

CLITTERHOUSE

Yes, I borrowed the gardener's ladder and forced the landing window.

ANN

With the scalpel?

CLITTERHOUSE

No, I used a table knife that time. I picked the lock with a bit of wire and forced the drawer with a tire lever.

ANN
(Rather seriously)

You *are* joking, aren't you, Doctor?

CLITTERHOUSE
(Tossing ether cloth onto desk)

Would you like to see the Challing—swag?

ANN
(Laughing)

Of course not. You haven't got it.

16

CLITTERHOUSE

On the contrary, my trouble is now to dispose of it. (*Rises, putting coat behind him on back of chair*) I hadn't really considered that problem. (*A bell rings in the hall.*)

ANN

(*Puts ether bottle on desk*)

Why, that's the day bell.

CLITTERHOUSE

See who it is, will you?

ANN

Yes, Doctor. (ANN *goes out.* CLITTERHOUSE *crosses to desk, closes the bag and puts the ether away in the cupboard.* ANN *returns.* CLITTERHOUSE *stands at end of couch*) Doctor, it's Inspector Charles!

CLITTERHOUSE

Who?

ANN

Inspector Charles!

CLITTERHOUSE

Good lord!

ANN

You were joking about those jewels, weren't you?

CLITTERHOUSE

Not a word to him, for heaven's sake! What does he want?

17

ANN

He just asked for you.

CLITTERHOUSE

Show him in. (ANN *exits.* CLITTERHOUSE *crosses to desk. He puts away bag in bottom drawer and manuscript book in top, and, standing at desk, is winding up bandage as* INSPECTOR CHARLES *enters.*)

ANN

Inspector Charles.

CHARLES
(Just inside)

Good evening, Doctor.

CLITTERHOUSE
(Cautiously)

Good evening, Inspector. (ANN *is watching tensely.*)

CHARLES

Well, how are you, old man? (*Crossing to* CLITTERHOUSE, *shakes his hand.*)

CLITTERHOUSE
(Relieved)

What's the idea, Charley?

CHARLES
(Takes off overcoat)

I saw a light in the hall, so I thought I'd ring the bell.

CLITTERHOUSE
(Sits on upper end of desk)

I thought this might be an official visit, or something.

18

CHARLES

Oh? ... What have you been up to? (*Throws overcoat on couch*) I thought he looked a bit funny when I came in—didn't he, Nurse?

ANN

(*Goes to coffee table*)

Oh! I didn't notice anything, Inspector.

CHARLES

(*Pats* CLITTERHOUSE's *shoulder*)

Well! How are you, anyway?

CLITTERHOUSE

Me? ... Oh ... Blood pressure's up at the moment, I think. ... What are you doing this way?

CHARLES

Just hanging about, you know. ... Who's in charge of the coffee?

CLITTERHOUSE

(*Crosses to* ANN, *looking into her face*)

Oh, Nurse! Another cup for Inspector Charles, please.

ANN

Yes, Doctor. (*Exits and leaves door open.*)

CLITTERHOUSE

You're a long way from the Yard, aren't you, Charley?

CHARLES

(*Coming to left of chair*)

And I'm a long way from my bed, Clit. ... Lousy life, a policeman's. (*Lifts the overcoat—to smell ether.*)

19

CLITTERHOUSE

(*Is closing door after* ANN. *Turns quickly*)
Here, I'll take that! (*Takes coat and puts it on couch.*)

CHARLES

I'll stay for a cup of coffee. Then I'll get out of your way.

CLITTERHOUSE

Don't hurry. I'm glad to see you! (ANN *enters with cup and saucer and goes to coffee table.*)

CHARLES

(*Sits on arm of chair*)
That's a lie! ... You've probably been out half the night, and you look dog tired.

CLITTERHOUSE

Oh, well, I think I'll have another cup of coffee, please, Nurse. (*Picks up cup from desk.*)

ANN

Yes, Doctor. (*Cup is on tray, plug in percolator.*)

CLITTERHOUSE

(*Moves round desk*)
And you have some too, Nurse ... I don't want to be left alone with a detective-inspector. (*Digs his shoulder in passing behind chair.*)

CHARLES

Ah, queer what a guilty conscience can do, isn't it, Nurse?
20

ANN
(*Steadily*)
Yes, Inspector.

CLITTERHOUSE
You don't say what you're doing over here, Charley.... Or is it a secret?

CHARLES
I'm supposed to be inquiring into that little bit of nocturnal thieving at Lady Challing's. (CLITTERHOUSE *is holding cup—turns to* ANN.)

ANN
(*Rises*)
Lady Challing's?

CLITTERHOUSE
(*Straightens up.* ANN *takes cup. Looks at him. Then sits again.*)
The third burglary, Nurse.

CHARLES
That's right.... The third burglary round here in a fortnight.... How did you know?

CLITTERHOUSE
Inside information, old boy!

CHARLES
Oh, of course—the newspapers!

CLITTERHOUSE
(*Moves close to* CHARLES)
Don't the local police usually handle that sort of thing?

CHARLES

Lady Challing's got rather a pull.... So the Yard's showing willing by sending me.

CLITTERHOUSE

Oh, and what are you doing about it?

CHARLES

I told you, just hanging around.... You see, we know those three jobs were done by the same man.

CLITTERHOUSE

How do you know?

CHARLES

Oh, by the style, as it were.... I'm really just waiting for him to do a fourth ... and then we'll probably get him.

ANN

You mean, you want to be on the spot, Inspector? (*Unplugs percolator.*)

CHARLES

Yes.... By the way, I told the constable on the beat that I might be in here—in case I'm wanted.

CLITTERHOUSE

Are you expecting another burglary tonight?

CHARLES

In a way.... The first three were done at four-day intervals. He'll do another soon....

22

THE AMAZING DR. CLITTERHOUSE

CLITTERHOUSE
(*Moving behind* ANN *to fireplace*)
Oh, will he?

CHARLES
Yes, one of the regular birds, this fellow—not that he'll be easy to net.

CLITTERHOUSE
You mean—he's clever?

CHARLES
I'll tell you how clever.... (ANN *crosses, hands* CHARLES *coffee, goes back to chair and sits down.*) Oh, thanks. On Lady Challing's job, this man took a ladder (CLITTERHOUSE *takes cigarette box from mantel, moves to coffee table*), which the gardener had left under the hedge, and got on to the garage roof with it.

CLITTERHOUSE
An opportunist.... (*Offers cigarette to* CHARLES.)

CHARLES
(*Taking cigarette*)
Thanks! Then he forced a landing window with a table knife —we know that by the "marks.".... He picked the lock on the library door, and forced the desk. (CLITTERHOUSE *turns and looks at* ANN, *then continues to walk to front of desk.*)

CLITTERHOUSE
What with?

CHARLES

I don't know. Something thin. (CLITTERHOUSE *strikes match on desk*) Jammed in between the top of the drawer and the woodwork.

CLITTERHOUSE

What about a tire lever, Charley? (*Looks at* ANN.)

CHARLES

Yes, that'd do it. (CLITTERHOUSE *lights his cigarette*) Oh! Thanks!

CLITTERHOUSE

(*Motioning in air with match alight*)

He could push it in . . . press the drawer down so that the tongue of the lock cleared, then pull the drawer out with the bent end of the lever. Quiet too. No splintering. (*Puts burnt match down in ash tray on desk.*)

CHARLES

That's about it. Something quite simple.

CLITTERHOUSE

(ANN *rises, moves slowly round with coffee*)

Tell me, Charley. Don't all these burglars use simple methods? (*Sits on edge of desk, facing* CHARLES) A table knife and a tire lever and a bit of bent wire. . . . Smart, you know.

CHARLES

Smart? The fellow was an absolute amateur!

CLITTERHOUSE

Amateur? . . . but you said . . . (ANN *crosses to chair and sits.*)

24

CHARLES

He climbed ladders and roofs, crept through the house and picked a lock—but the library window, the very room he wanted to get into, was undone all the time.

CLITTERHOUSE

But perhaps he didn't know that!

CHARLES

A clever crook would have looked around first.... And if he had to open a window, why climb on a roof to do it?

CLITTERHOUSE

Perhaps the landing one was easier.

CHARLES

No. The library one was easier—if he'd known about it.

ANN

Would you have said this burglar was—inexperienced, Inspector?

CHARLES

A raw amateur!

CLITTERHOUSE

I see....

ANN

(*Rises, goes to* CHARLES)

Oh! More coffee, Inspector?

CHARLES

No, thank you.

ANN

What about you, Doctor? (*Moving round to him.*)

CLITTERHOUSE

Coffee? ... No, no coffee. Thank you! (*Rises, puts cup on coffee tray.*)

ANN
(*Crosses to desk. Makes notes*)
Did this ... burglar get away with very much, Inspector?

CHARLES

Quite a bit. ... Lady Challing had a diamond necklet—thing like a dog-collar. He got that. ... She says it's worth two thousand pounds.

CLITTERHOUSE
(*Turning interestedly*)
And is it?

CHARLES

No. ...

CLITTERHOUSE

Oh. ... (*Turning fireside chair round close to* CHARLES) Tell me, Charley, how do these burglars get *rid* of their swag?

CHARLES

Break it up, or use a fence.

CLITTERHOUSE

Fence? ... You mean a receiver?
26

CHARLES

(*Turns in chair toward* CLITTERHOUSE)

Yes, but we've got tabs on most of them. You see, this fellow will probably try and pawn his stuff.... Then we'll drop on him like a cartload of bricks.

CLITTERHOUSE

(*Laughs*)

Ha! Ha! But perhaps he won't pawn it....

CHARLES

(*Laughs*)

Ha! Ha! We'll get him—even if he does go to a fence.

ANN

(*Does not look up. Still making notes*)

How?

CHARLES

Why, the fence would give him away—split on him, just to try and prove to us that he never does take stolen property!

CLITTERHOUSE

Oh! You mean, double-cross him?

CHARLES

Yes, a fence won't take chances with anyone he doesn't know.

CLITTERHOUSE

Are they all like that?

CHARLES

Pretty well.

27

CLITTERHOUSE
(*Casually*)
Tell me, Charley, who would you call a *good* fence?

CHARLES
They're all bad!

CLITTERHOUSE
All the same?

CHARLES
More or less.... Nothing smart about any of them—bar one.

CLITTERHOUSE
Oh! Who's that?

CHARLES
Oh, a fellow called Kellerman—Benny Kellerman.

CLITTERHOUSE
Kellerman....

CHARLES
Yes. He's behind a hell of a lot of stealing.... (*Leans forward*) This is between ourselves, Clit!

CLITTERHOUSE
Of course...and we can trust Nurse Ann....Can't we, Nurse?

ANN
(*Folding and closing blood pressure apparatus. Steadily*)
Yes...Doctor...

CHARLES

Yes, we've been after Kellerman, time and again, but he's a leery bird.

CLITTERHOUSE

He is, eh?

CHARLES

He used to be a working jeweler and watchmaker, then he got into trouble. . . . Now he runs one of those little clubs . . .

CLITTERHOUSE

You told me about them. Is his in the East End?

CHARLES

No, off Theobalds Road. (*The telephone bell rings.* ANN *lifts the receiver.*)

ANN

Hello? . . . Yes. . . . Yes, he is here. . . . It's for you, Inspector.

CHARLES

Me? Oh! Thank you. (*Rises, takes receiver from* ANN *across desk.* ANN *takes blood pressure apparatus to cabinet*) Inspector Charles here. How did you? . . . Oh, you called the constable up in the police box, did you? . . . You're too clever, Sergeant! What d'you want? . . . What! (ANN *turns, looks at* CLITTERHOUSE) . . . Well, I'll be damned! Yes, at once! Good-bye. (*Replaces receiver. Turns to* CLITTERHOUSE) What did I tell you?

CLITTERHOUSE
(*Rises*)

Your amateur burglar again!

CHARLES

You're right. . . . Cranston Lodge— (*Puts cigarette out*) —at Councillor Duckett's place. I must be off, old boy. (*Turns for coat.* ANN *goes to door.*)

CLITTERHOUSE
(*Crosses to couch. Picks up coat*)
Won't you finish your coffee?

CHARLES

Yes, it's too good to leave. . . . (*Drinks, puts cup on desk.*)

CLITTERHOUSE

So he's pulled off another job right under your very nose! (*Helps him on.*)

CHARLES

Yes, but he'll slip up. . . . Amateurs always do. (CLITTERHOUSE *hands hat*) Well, so long. (*Crosses to door.*)

CLITTERHOUSE

So long, Charley!

CHARLES
(*Turns at door*)
I may be around here for a bit, off and on. . . . Good night, old boy.

CLITTERHOUSE

Good night. . . .
(CHARLES *exits with* ANN. CLITTERHOUSE *then crosses to desk and sits down. Takes book from top drawer, opens it as* ANN *re-enters.*)

ANN

(*A step or two from door*)

There *has* been a burglary at Councillor Duckett's house!

CLITTERHOUSE

And you've seen the proceeds.

ANN

(*Crosses to above chair*)

Yes. But you ... you can't be the inspector's burglar?

CLITTERHOUSE

I should be if he caught me. (*Chuckles*) I wish we could have taken my blood pressure when he walked in here.

ANN

Do you mean that you've really and truly stolen these things?

CLITTERHOUSE

Four burglaries inside a fortnight and he calls me an amateur.

ANN

Four ... *burglaries!* ... Doctor ... you can't realize what you're doing!

CLITTERHOUSE

I think I've a pretty good idea, Nurse. ...

ANN

But you can't have ... What can you possibly want that jewelry for?

CLITTERHOUSE

Listen, Nurse...

ANN

Doctor, if you were caught...

CLITTERHOUSE

That would be awkward, wouldn't it?

ANN

Surely you realize how...awkward! It would be terrible!

CLITTERHOUSE

You know, I have a very good reason for all this....

ANN

But you can't have. There's no excuse for *burglary*—for *stealing!*

CLITTERHOUSE
(Sits back)

I don't look at it quite like that!...You see, I've grown rather tired of all this "Well-how-are-you-today?—Worse-thank-you-Doctor!"

ANN

But you've a wonderful practice!

CLITTERHOUSE

Yes! And I can go on having it until I'm old and gray and doddery. But I believe I'm on to something that's very much worth while. Something that might prove more important than my practice.

ANN

More ... important!

CLITTERHOUSE

Yes, more important! (*Rises*) You see, knowing old Charley, I've grown rather interested in this sort of thing. (*Goes between coffee table and chair to mantel*) Not in police work exactly, but in crime and—crooks. (*Takes pipe and pouch from mantel.*)

ANN

You mean you are experimenting about crooks, then?

CLITTERHOUSE
(*Filling pipe*)

But I'm being one, dammit! You see old Charley believes that the best way to cure crime is to catch the crooks quickly and tuck them away behind bars.... My idea is that you've got to start long before that!

ANN

Do you mean ... start psychologically?

CLITTERHOUSE

No ... no, no! ... Nurse ... Has it ever occurred to you to wonder why criminal activities should actually change a man's face and physique.... Gradually change someone who was once quite normal into something furtive and cringing.... It does, you know, in time!

ANN

I'm afraid I've never thought about anything like that....

33

CLITTERHOUSE

But that's what I'm after—the pathology of crime, Nurse! ... There are medical reasons for those changes.... They affect the mentality of a crook and influence his actions.... They are the result of the fear and excitement and the tense emotions which he undergoes.... (*Puts pouch on desk*) And I want to find out the precise nature of those reactions.... I can do it only by studying crooks while they are actually at work—not after Charley has stuck 'em away behind bars! (*Takes matches from desk*) It's research work and I needed a living subject ... so I started experiments on myself.... (*Lights pipe.*)

ANN

I don't ... quite understand you, Doctor.

CLITTERHOUSE

I planned a burglary, I carried it through ... as accurately as I could, I observed my own reactions ... pulse, respiration, blood pressure....

ANN

And that is what you were doing tonight?

CLITTERHOUSE

Yes, my fourth ... experiment ... I believe I'm discovering something. (*Pauses, sits in desk chair*) It's very fascinating.

ANN

But, Doctor, have you thought of the risk you're running?

CLITTERHOUSE

It's worth it ... well worth it, if what I learn helps— In the way I think it may.... Only I didn't intend to involve anybody else in this....

34

ANN

But, now I've seen what's in your bag ...

CLITTERHOUSE

I had to explain. Only it needn't concern you and it won't affect our work here.

ANN

You think it won't? I don't like it.

CLITTERHOUSE

I'm sorry if I've upset you, Nurse.... But I must go on with it.

ANN

Yes ... but I wish I could stop you. (*Pause. He looks through book.*)

ANN
(*Turns*)

Doctor ... have you been thinking about this for very long?

CLITTERHOUSE

Oh! Quite some time.

ANN

Isn't it possible you have it all in the wrong perspective? (*Pause.*)

CLITTERHOUSE
(*Looks up*)

Are you hinting that I've gone slightly mental?

35

ANN

Well, you have been overworking.

CLITTERHOUSE

Nurse, I know precisely what I'm doing. . . . It is simply research work—in a slightly unusual form. .

ANN

A very unusual form, Doctor.

CLITTERHOUSE

Well . . . if you think that, Nurse—you'd better go home to bed.

ANN

Yes, Doctor. (*He starts writing. She takes cup from desk and crosses to coffee table. Picks up tray and goes, then turns.*) I hope I haven't annoyed you, Doctor.

CLITTERHOUSE
(*Looks up*)
Humoring the mental patient, Nurse?

ANN

I . . . I do feel a little concerned.

CLITTERHOUSE

Nurse, I know precisely what I'm doing. Don't you worry about me, I'm quite all right. Good night. . . .

ANN

Good night, Doctor. (*Turns to door and exits.*)
36

CLITTERHOUSE
(Loudly)

Nurse!

ANN
(Off stage)

Yes? *(Re-enters, without tray.)*

CLITTERHOUSE

Were you thinking of telephoning Sir James Hillery in the morning?

ANN

Telephoning, Doctor?

CLITTERHOUSE

You were, weren't you?

ANN

What makes you think that?

CLITTERHOUSE

Well, we called him in when old Trimmer began to see things the wrong way. Don't do it, Nurse!

ANN

But I feel that someone should.... *(He rises, crosses to* ANN *before speaking.)*

CLITTERHOUSE

Nurse! You said that I could trust you! ... This is a professional matter, and *very* confidential.

ANN

Yes, Doctor.

37

CLITTERHOUSE

And if this jewelry worries you ... I shall be taking a walk down Theobalds Road tomorrow, to see Benny Kellerman. (*Crosses back to desk chair*) Good night. ...

ANN

Good night ... Doctor. ... (ANN *exits*. CLITTERHOUSE *watches the door close. He squares himself to his work and begins to write.*)

Curtain

ACT ONE

Scene II

SCENE: KELLERMAN'S CLUB, *off Theobalds Road, at ten o'clock the following evening.*

KELLERMAN *is behind the bar, the flap of which is down.* DAISY *is standing at bar, smoking.* PAL GREEN *is standing at door.* ALL *are looking toward the door. Knock on door.* KELLERMAN *speaks as he comes round bar. He puts flap down again. Goes to door, rolling up his sleeves.*

KELLERMAN

All right. Stand away, Pal, I'll see who it is.

PAL

It's coppers!

DAISY

Coppers don't knock like that.

PAL

Some of these new 'uns would. (*Knocking on door.*)

KELLERMAN
(*Shouting*)

All right, all right. (*Glancing at* DAISY) O.K.? (*Knocking comes again.*)

DAISY

Yes ... go on. (KELLERMAN *throws open the hatch in the door, revealing the face of* CLITTERHOUSE.)

39

KELLERMAN

What's all the blarney about?

CLITTERHOUSE

I was beginning to think there was no one here. I knocked three times.

KELLERMAN

We heard you! ... What d'you want?

CLITTERHOUSE

Benny Kellerman.

KELLERMAN

That's me. ...

CLITTERHOUSE

Oh, indeed? ... Well, then you're the man I want to see.

KELLERMAN

Who are you?

CLITTERHOUSE

I can't talk to you from outside here.

KELLERMAN

Who sent you?

CLITTERHOUSE

Why ... Inspector Charles, of Scotland Yard. (KELLERMAN *looks at* DAISY.)

40

PAL

(*Quickly sits in chair behind table*)
I told you! A rozzer!

DAISY

You keep quiet, Pal. . . .

KELLERMAN

Oh! Ho!! Copper, are you? . . . Come on in. . . . (*Closes panel, opens door.* CLITTERHOUSE *enters, raises his hat to* DAISY. KELLERMAN *shuts and bolts door, then to* CLITTERHOUSE) Why didn't you say that at first, mister?

CLITTERHOUSE

Say what?

KELLERMAN

That you was a copper. You didn't knock like one.

DAISY

One knock—and they usually start kicking!

PAL

(*Rises*)
Are you one o' these new pansy police, mate? . . . The college kind!

CLITTERHOUSE

I'm afraid there's a misapprehension, Mister—Kellerman— I am not a policeman.

KELLERMAN

You just told me you was.

41

CLITTERHOUSE

Oh, no ... I heard of you through Inspector Charles of Scotland Yard.

KELLERMAN

And you're not a copper?

CLITTERHOUSE

No. ...

KELLERMAN
(*Angrily*)
Then what the hell d' you want?

CLITTERHOUSE

Well, as a matter of fact, I want to do a little business with you.

KELLERMAN

What kind of business?

CLITTERHOUSE

Confidential ...

PAL

Tell him he's butting in, Benny! (*Turns to table, picks up paper and sits on edge of table.* DAISY *goes up to slot machine.*)

KELLERMAN

I've got no business, bar running this club.

CLITTERHOUSE

Charley told me that you had.

42

KELLERMAN

Never mind what he said—I haven't! . . . See? (DAISY *works slot machine.*)

CLITTERHOUSE

Well. (*Crosses to bar*) Let's have a drink.

KELLERMAN

I don't serve anybody, bar members.

CLITTERHOUSE

(*Turns to* DAISY. *Takes hat off. A step from bar*)
Excuse me, but—is this lady a member?

DAISY

(*Turns from slot machine*)
I don't know what you want—but don't try and drag me in it. (*Sits on bench near alcove and reads a magazine.*)

KELLERMAN

(*Crossing to* CLITTERHOUSE)
Are you a friend of Inspector Charles?

CLITTERHOUSE

Yes, but he doesn't know I've come here, and I have nothing to do with the police.

KELLERMAN

I'm not afraid of the police!

CLITTERHOUSE

I didn't suspect for one moment that you were.

43

PAL

(*Looking into his paper*)

Tell him to hop it, Benny!

CLITTERHOUSE

At the same time it's rather a pity to allow prejudice to stand in the way of business, Mister Kellerman.

KELLERMAN

There's no business you and me can do.

CLITTERHOUSE

Oh! That's a pity.... Well, let's drink to old Charley. (PAL *looks up.*)

KELLERMAN

I don't like the feller.

CLITTERHOUSE

Then let's drink to each other.

DAISY

Are you paying?

CLITTERHOUSE

Of course.

DAISY

(*Rises. Goes to table and sits in chair*)

Come on, Benny, let's have a drink before he goes.... Mine's a Martini—dry. (KELLERMAN *crosses front of* CLITTERHOUSE *and round into bar. Leaves flap up.*)

44

CLITTERHOUSE
(*At bar*)

Oh! Do you serve Martinis here? I'll join you. (PAL *coughs meaningfully. To* PAL) What's yours, sir?

PAL

Well, if it's free ... mine's a pig's-ear—beer to you, Guv'nor! (*Goes to table with paper.*)

CLITTERHOUSE

Two dry Martinis and a pig's-ear. You'll join us, won't you? (*Puts hat on counter.*)

KELLERMAN

I don't mind if I do ... (*Over shoulder*) ... but this don't mean anything, you know. (*He busies himself over the drinks.*)

CLITTERHOUSE
(*Turning toward* DAISY)

You know, I had great difficulty in finding this place.

DAISY

You've got to know the way ...

CLITTERHOUSE

Old Charley just happened to mention that it was off Theobalds Road ... I've been wandering up and down for over two hours. (KELLERMAN *has now two Martinis and beer on counter. Beer is not opened and has glass inverted over neck. He pours whisky for himself.*)

DAISY

Hear that, Benny?

45

PAL

You must ha' wanted to see Benny pretty bad. (KELLERMAN *comes out from behind bar.*)

CLITTERHOUSE

I did rather.... You know, Old Charley regards you as the best man in London at your business. (PAL *and* DAISY *turn round.*)

KELLERMAN

What business?

CLITTERHOUSE

Running this club.

DAISY

Here, are you on the crook? (KELLERMAN *comes round bar to table with beer and one Martini.*)

CLITTERHOUSE

Are you?

DAISY

I asked you ...

CLITTERHOUSE

Mr. Kellerman isn't, is he?

PAL

(*Laughing*)

Hear that, Benny? That's good, that is. (KELLERMAN *glares at* PAL *and slams bottle on table.*)

PAL
(*Sheepishly*)
Thanks, mate.

KELLERMAN
(*Putting down* DAISY'S *glass*)
Here's yours, Daisy.

DAISY
Thanks, Benny. (KELLERMAN *goes past* CLITTERHOUSE *to bar.*)

CLITTERHOUSE
(*As* KELLERMAN *passes him*)
Mr. Kellerman ... (*Raising glass*) ... to our better acquaintance ... (*To* DAISY) and to you, sir ... (*To* PAL) good luck ...

PAL
(*Has poured beer, now raises hat in toast*)
Rot him! (*Drinks with hat raised.*)

CLITTERHOUSE
Excuse me, but what does he mean by "rot him"? (*Laughing.* KELLERMAN *drinks.*)

DAISY
That's for the judge. He sent Pal up for a three-year stretch. ... He's never got over it.

PAL
Innocent I was, mate—innocent as a new-born babe. They hung it on me.

CLITTERHOUSE

Bad luck, Pal.

DAISY

Cheerio! (CLITTERHOUSE *and* DAISY *drink.*)

KELLERMAN

Did you say you heard about me from Inspector Charles?

CLITTERHOUSE

(*Turns to bar*)

Yes ... only by chance. ... Excuse me, but is it all right to discuss business with ... others present?

DAISY

Don't you mind us! (*Commences to gather cards.*)

PAL

You go ahead, mate. (*Leans back, lights cigarette.*)

KELLERMAN

What do you want?

CLITTERHOUSE

Well, I understand that, at times, and under certain circumstances, of course. ... You do undertake to dispose of ... shall we say ... articles of jewelry that ...

KELLERMAN

(*Puts glass on bar*)

Come on. Out with it! ... What are you trying to say?

CLITTERHOUSE

Simply that I've got something to sell.

48

PAL

Blimey—and I thought you was a flattie!

DAISY

Benny don't buy from strangers.

KELLERMAN

Benny don't buy at all.

CLITTERHOUSE
(*Turns back to him*)

No. But *if* you did—and *if* I had something to sell, what would be the first move?

PAL

He'd buy on the "Hue and Cry." (*Drinks.*)

CLITTERHOUSE
(*Turning*)

The "You and Who"?

KELLERMAN
(*Behind bar*)

"Police Gazette."

DAISY

According to their valuing.... (*Turns in chair to him*) Here, are you coming the old soldier with us? (KELLERMAN *has turned away, polishing glass.*)

CLITTERHOUSE

No...I don't think so.

PAL
(*Finishing drink, rises*)
I still got an idea he's a nark, Benny.

CLITTERHOUSE
I'm not a nark and I'm not coming the old soldier. I've got, er—a daffy of sparklers and I want to flash them. (KELLERMAN *and* PAL *turn*) Is that plain?

· DAISY
Yes, but it don't sound natural....

CLITTERHOUSE
No, it doesn't sound very natural to me either. (*Turns to* KELLERMAN) This "Police Gazette"... Have you, by any chance, the latest copy? (KELLERMAN *produces a copy of the* "Police Gazette." CLITTERHOUSE *looks through it.*)

DAISY
What do you make of him, Pal?

PAL
He seems to have the patter all right.

DAISY
He might have got it out of a book.

PAL
You can't get that stuff out of a book.

CLITTERHOUSE
(*Looking through paper on bar*)
I don't know whether what I want is here.... Yes, here it is
50

...diamond necklet...platinum brooch set with emeralds....
Have a look at this, will you. (*Turns "Gazette" on bar to*
KELLERMAN.)

DAISY
(*Rises, goes to him*)
You're not going to tell me you've done a job....

CLITTERHOUSE
(*Turns, smiling*)
I'm not going to tell you anything at all. (*She shrugs her
shoulders, steps to lower end of bar.*)

KELLERMAN
(*Tapping "Gazette"*)
Is this the stuff that you say you've got?

CLITTERHOUSE
(*To* KELLERMAN)
What does the paper say it's worth?

KELLERMAN
Two thousand seven hundred...

PAL
Blimey! You pulled off a good 'un, mate.... You working
single-handed?

CLITTERHOUSE
(*Turns to* PAL)
Perhaps I wasn't working at all. (*Drinks. Not understanding,
but chancing it*) Er.... No.... (*To* KELLERMAN, *as he puts
glass down*) If you were buying that stuff, what would you
pay for it?

51

KELLERMAN

Are you asking me if I buy stolen property?

CLITTERHOUSE

I am. . . .

KELLERMAN

Well, I don't. See! (*Puts* CLITTERHOUSE's *glass in front of him with a bang*) Now then finish your drink and get out. (*Pause.* PAL *turns slowly away.*)

CLITTERHOUSE

Is that your last word? (KELLERMAN *puts "Gazette" away, turns his back and wipes glass.* CLITTERHOUSE *picks up hat and turns away slowly.*)

DAISY

Benny's leery, see? . . . He don't know you.

KELLERMAN

I don't know what you're talking about. . . . Coming in here an' offering me jewelry out o' the "Hue and Cry"! . . . What d'you think I am?

CLITTERHOUSE

I haven't offered you anything. I simply asked.

PAL
(*Behind him*)

Show him the stuff, mate. . . . (KELLERMAN *comes from behind bar, closes flap, and places whisky bottle on it.*)

CLITTERHOUSE

D'you think I carry it about with me?

52

KELLERMAN

You've been asking a lot o' funny questions, you have. And I don't like ... (*There is a knock on the door, followed by a kick which makes it rattle.* CLITTERHOUSE *finishes drink. Puts on hat.*)

VOICE

Open up there!

PAL

This is the cops, this time. (*Grabs paper from table. Sits at table and puts feet on chair.*)

KELLERMAN

Stand away from that bar ... (CLITTERHOUSE *steps away from bar.* DAISY *sits near table.* KELLERMAN *goes quickly to the door and opens hatch*) Hello, Sergeant!

SERGEANT

Come on. Open up. (KELLERMAN *unbolts door, throwing it wide. Two* PLAINCLOTHES POLICEMEN *step inside.* SERGEANT *signs* POLICEMEN *to guard other door.* KELLERMAN *closes door, then goes to* SERGEANT) Who have you got here? Daisy! Pal Green! Who's that?

DAISY

A friend of mine.

SERGEANT

Where's Bob Oakes?

KELLERMAN

Who?

SERGEANT

You heard!...Have a look out the back.

CONSTABLE

Yes, Sergeant. (CONSTABLE *hurries out through the door by the bar.*)

SERGEANT

Oakie's been here.

KELLERMAN

Not tonight.

SERGEANT

No?...Well, I want him. (*He has picked up whisky bottle on flap of bar.* DAISY *watches him.*)

DAISY

(*Looking down at cards*)

Have a drink, Sergeant.

SERGEANT

(*Realizing he is holding bottle, puts it down*)

Don't be saucy! (*Gives cursory look behind bar.*)

DAISY

Well, I only asked....

KELLERMAN

Oh! Shut up, Daisy.

CONSTABLE

(*Returning*)

Nothing out there, Sergeant.

SERGEANT

Sure?

CONSTABLE

There's no one in the room there and the door in the yard's bolted. (CLITTERHOUSE *crosses slowly to* DAISY.)

SERGEANT

He could have climbed the wall, couldn't he?

CONSTABLE

He'd have had to stand on something, and there's nothing there.

SERGEANT
(*To* DAISY)

Did one of you help him over?

DAISY

Benny told you Oakie hasn't been here.

SERGEANT

When did you see him last?

KELLERMAN

Oh! Er. . . . Three or four days ago. (CLITTERHOUSE *plays a card for* DAISY. *She looks at him and smiles.*)

SERGEANT
(*Pauses, goes over to* PAL)

Have you seen him?

PAL
(*With great innocence*)

Me, Sergeant?

SERGEANT

Yes.

PAL

No, Sergeant. Not for nigh on three weeks, Sergeant. He's got a job at Brighton, Oakie has.... Going straight, he is!

SERGEANT

Yes! As straight as Harry Lauder's walking stick!

DAISY

(*Not looking at him*)

What do you want him for?

SERGEANT

(*Turns*)

Yes, I'd be likely to tell you, wouldn't I?

DAISY

Oakie hasn't done *anything!* (CLITTERHOUSE *goes back to bar.*)

SERGEANT

We've just a few questions to ask him, that's all.

KELLERMAN

(*Turns to* SERGEANT)

What about?

SERGEANT

Never mind what about.... D'you know where he was last night?

56

KELLERMAN

I do.... *And* he wasn't up to anything.

SERGEANT

Sure?

KELLERMAN

I know it.

SERGEANT

Well, somebody's pulled off a job that was just his hand-writing.... If it wasn't him, he can come to the station and say so.... If it was him, we'll pick him up anyway. (*During this speech,* CLITTERHOUSE *notices beer running under bar. Crosses slowly down toward it.* SERGEANT, *watching him, steps pace to him.* CLITTERHOUSE *stops and leans against bar. Whole business very unobtrusive.*)

DAISY

It wasn't Oakie, I'll swear to that.

PAL

What was the job, Sergeant?

SERGEANT
(*Turns to* PAL)

It's jewelry.... (*Turns to* KELLERMAN) Kellerman, it's stuff that's red hot ... understand me?

KELLERMAN
(*Blandly innocent*)

No, Sergeant.

57

SERGEANT

You wouldn't, would you? (KELLERMAN *puts finger in his mouth, cleaning his gums*) But I'm telling you, it'll burn the fingers of anybody that touches it.

KELLERMAN

(*Takes finger out, looks at it, then speaks*)
What is it?

SERGEANT

Nearly two thousand pounds' worth.... (KELLERMAN *whistles*) Pearl necklace, diamond bracelet, brooches and rings, all very nice stuff.

CLITTERHOUSE

Taken from St. John's Wood way, Sergeant? (ALL *look at* CLITTERHOUSE *who is leaning back, both elbows on bar.*)

SERGEANT

How did you know that?

CLITTERHOUSE

I read the papers.

SERGEANT

Oh, you do.... Well, who are you?

CLITTERHOUSE

I beg your pardon?

SERGEANT

You heard.... What's your name?

58

CLITTERHOUSE

Well! For the matter of that, what is yours?

SERGEANT

Don't try and be funny with me! ... Come on, answer up!
Who are you?

CLITTERHOUSE

Well, who are you?

SERGEANT

Sergeant Bates is my name. ...

CLITTERHOUSE

Oh? Have you got your warrant card?

SERGEANT

(PAL *sits up, leans over, listening*)

What d'you mean?

CLITTERHOUSE

You know perfectly well what I mean. ... Your warrant
card will prove you're bona fide. ... Have you got one?

SERGEANT

Of course I have!

CLITTERHOUSE

Do you mind if I see it?

SERGEANT

(*Crosses slowly*)

Here, what's your game? (CLITTERHOUSE *does not move.*
CONSTABLE *half steps in.* KELLERMAN *comes nearer.*)

59

CLITTERHOUSE

Well, you come in here asking questions of everyone, and we have a right to know who you are!

SERGEANT

They know me here.

CLITTERHOUSE

All the same I should like to see your card.

SERGEANT

Very well. (*He truculently sticks card into* CLITTERHOUSE'S *face.* PAL *rises.*)

CLITTERHOUSE

(*He looks at it, but makes no attempt to touch it. Reading calmly*)

Sergeant, Percival Horace Bates. (PAL *laughs. Sits quickly.* SERGEANT *turns on him,* PAL *hastily reads paper.*)

SERGEANT

(*Card in* CLITTERHOUSE'S *face again*)

Finished?

CLITTERHOUSE

Thank you....

SERGEANT

(*Puts card away*)

Now then, who are you?

CLITTERHOUSE

What's that to do with you?

60

SERGEANT

I asked your name. . . .

CLITTERHOUSE

And I refuse to give it.

SERGEANT

Don't come that with me!

CLITTERHOUSE

You have no shadow of right even in requesting my name.

SERGEANT

Oh! Haven't I?

CLITTERHOUSE

No!

SERGEANT

Oh! (SERGEANT *turns, sees* DAISY *in act of drinking. Looks at* KELLERMAN) How long does your license go?

KELLERMAN

Ten thirty, Sergeant.

SERGEANT
(*To* CONSTABLE)

What's the time?

CONSTABLE
(*Looking at watch*)

Eleven minutes past ten.

SERGEANT
(*Turning to* CLITTERHOUSE)
I've a good mind to pick you up, anyway.

CLITTERHOUSE
On what grounds?

SERGEANT
Suspicion. . . .

CLITTERHOUSE
Then why not do it, Sergeant? If you have anything to be suspicious about.

SERGEANT
Have *you* seen Oakie?

CLITTERHOUSE
I don't even know him.

SERGEANT
(*Close to him*)
Very well then. But you keep a civil tongue in your head the next time you speak to a police officer. You'll get yourself into trouble before you've done. (*Taps* CLITTERHOUSE *on chest.*)

CLITTERHOUSE
(*Flicking imaginary dirt*)
I think you're more likely to do that, Sergeant. Good night. (*Turns to bar.*)

SERGEANT
I'll remember you. (KELLERMAN *opens door.*)

62

CLITTERHOUSE

Quite right. (SERGEANT *crosses to door*) Oh! And Sergeant (*He crosses to* SERGEANT) if this kind of impertinence is repeated, I shall take steps to bring it to the notice of your superiors at the Yard. Good night. (*Crosses back to bar.* SERGEANT *is speechless.*)

SERGEANT
(*To* CONSTABLE)

Oh, come on. (*He exits.* CONSTABLE *looks over his shoulder at* CLITTERHOUSE *as he exits. The door slams behind them.* KELLERMAN *bolts it.* PAL *and* DAISY *are laughing, even* KELLERMAN *is smiling.*)

PAL

Blimey, did you hear that! "Take steps to bring it to the notice o' your superiors at the Yard!" (CLITTERHOUSE *has a quick look over bar, knowing* OAKIE *must be somewhere there.*)

DAISY

The way you choked the sergeant off! ...

KELLERMAN
(*Crossing to back of bar, picking up glasses and bottle from table*)

He'll have it in for me, after this!

PAL
(*Rises, slaps* CLITTERHOUSE *on back*)

Good on you, mate! Benny, he's a right 'un. (KELLERMAN *stops, turns, then continues to bar.*)

63

DAISY

You've certainly got a nerve.... What is your name?

CLITTERHOUSE

(*Smiling*)

I wouldn't even tell a policeman that. (*Stoops at the front of the bar, and bangs on the panel*) All right, Oakie, you can come out now.

KELLERMAN

How the hell did you know he was there? (OAKIE *emerges from beneath the bar, bringing a half-empty glass.*)

OAKIE

(*Laughing*)

I heard every word. Blimey, you're hot stuff, you are, mate.

CLITTERHOUSE

Your beer rather gave you away.... I could see it running out underneath the panel. (KELLERMAN *closes panel.*)

OAKIE

You don't think I was going to lose my drink for any blinkin' copper, do you? We thought you was a copper when you knocked first.

CLITTERHOUSE

So that's why you ducked in there. Well, put that down and have another.

OAKIE

Thanks. I'll finish this first.... (*Drinks. Puts glass on bar.*)

PAL

He's a right 'un, ain't he, Oakie?

OAKIE

Right 'un? I'll take me oath on it. What's the matter with you, Benny? I bet you never heard anybody tell a cop off like that before. (*Throws dart in board, then goes to cigarette machine and gets a packet from it.*)

KELLERMAN

No, I never did.... It was cool, I give you that credit.

PAL
(*Laughing*)

"Take steps to bring it to the notice of your superiors!" ... Gaw lummy, that was worth living for!

DAISY

You've tickled Pal.

CLITTERHOUSE

I have, haven't I?

OAKIE
(*Coming above table to* DAISY)

Yes. And he'd tickle you too, if you gave him half a chance.

DAISY

Oh, shut up! (THEY *all laugh.*)

OAKIE

Going to have another, China?

65

CLITTERHOUSE

Oh, no, this is on me. Same again, all round. What's for you, Oakie?

OAKIE

I'll have the same as you. (*To* PAL) It was lucky I stayed in there, Pal—I nearly came out.

KELLERMAN
(*Pouring drinks*)
'Ere, Oakie. You never did that job, did you?

OAKIE

No. Worse luck. Not me, but I wasn't anxious to answer any questions tonight.

CLITTERHOUSE

You know I'm afraid I owe you an apology, Oakie.

OAKIE
(*Crosses to* CLITTERHOUSE)
Whatever you've done, China, I forgive you. You're the right art, you are. (*Stretches out hand to shake.* CLITTERHOUSE' *puts glass in it.*)

CLITTERHOUSE

But I happen to know that you didn't do that job at St. John's Wood.

DAISY

We know he didn't, too.

KELLERMAN

D'you know who *did* do it?

66

CLITTERHOUSE

Yes.... (*Takes glasses from bar.*)

DAISY

Don't say it was you!

CLITTERHOUSE
(*Smiling*)

Well, if I did, you wouldn't believe me. Yours, Daisy. (*He puts glass in front of her, also takes* PAL's *beer. Passes beer bottle across table. It is unopened and has glass on top as before*) Here you are, Pal. (*Turns to bar, raising own glass*) Oakie, to your continued freedom!

OAKIE

'Ere, that don't sound too healthy—however, here's looking at you, China.

CLITTERHOUSE

Daisy!...

DAISY

Cheerio!!

CLITTERHOUSE

Mr. Kellerman, to the improvement of our relations. Pal, good luck.

PAL
(*Raises hat, as before*)

Rot him! (*All drink.* KELLERMAN *comes to end of bar.*)

67

KELLERMAN
(*With glass*)
You know, I can't make you out. (DAISY *sets cards for patience.*)

OAKIE
No. It strikes me he's about as careful as you are, Benny....
But you can talk to me, China!

CLITTERHOUSE
I believe I can, Oakie....

OAKIE
(*Snapping fingers*)
Have you, er, got something to sell?

CLITTERHOUSE
Maybe I have, and maybe I haven't.... (*Gesturing as* OAKIE
would) I'm saying nothing.

OAKIE
(*Smiling*)
All right, please yourself . . . no offense.

CLITTERHOUSE
(*Turning to bar*)
Have you got that "Gazette" again—and the one before it?

KELLERMAN
Yes!

DAISY
Going to make Benny price the stuff? (KELLERMAN *hands
him "Gazette."*)

CLITTERHOUSE

Something like that. (*Crosses to table, looks at "Gazette."*)

KELLERMAN

Here's the other one.

CLITTERHOUSE

Let's see. This is the one we talked about earlier.... May
I see the other copy? (*Puts one "Gazette" on table.* KELLERMAN
hands him the other one.)

PAL

Have you got something else in there, mate?

CLITTERHOUSE

(*Looking through it*)
My friends at the Yard may have flattered me.... Ah!

OAKIE

Is this yours? (*Pointing at first paper.* DAISY *looks over*
CLITTERHOUSE'S *shoulder.*)

CLITTERHOUSE

Well, I have an interest in it.... (*To* KELLERMAN) What
do you make the total there? (*Passes "Gazette" to* KELLERMAN,
pointing to particular paragraph.)

DAISY

You mean, you did that job as well? (*Now looking over*
KELLERMAN'S *shoulder.*)

KELLERMAN

Four hundred and seventy quid.

69

CLITTERHOUSE

And the sergeant assessed that haul last night at St. John's Wood at two thousand pounds, didn't he? (*Picks up first "Gazette" and takes out fountain pen. Writing on "Gazette" on knee*) That's two thousand four hundred and seventy pounds.... Plus that one in the first "Gazette."... Two thousand seven hundred. That makes five thousand one hundred and seventy quid.

PAL

Blimey! You're talking money, mate!

OAKIE

Are you on all that?

CLITTERHOUSE

(*Rather offhand about this "small" job*)
And there was another quite small job at about four hundred, I should think.... That makes four jobs at something like five thousand five hundred pounds— (*Looks up*) "Police Gazette" prices.

DAISY

You haven't done all those jobs, have you? (CLITTERHOUSE *turns to her.*)

OAKIE

After what he said to that copper, I'd given him credit for anything!

DAISY

Have you?

70

CLITTERHOUSE
(*To* DAISY)
Well, to be perfectly frank with you, Daisy, I have!

PAL
Gorn! You're kidding!

OAKIE
You mean it! Honest Injun, working on your own?

CLITTERHOUSE
(*Again guessing meaning*)
Yes.... (*There is a pause.*)

KELLERMAN
'Ere, Oakie, d' you think he's all right?

OAKIE
Well, you got to decide that for yourself, Benny.

CLITTERHOUSE
(*To* KELLERMAN)
Well, are you prepared to do business, Mr. Kellerman?

KELLERMAN
Here, that job the sergeant came about! ... Was that yours?

CLITTERHOUSE
Well, I seem to have copied Oakie's excellent handwriting.

OAKIE
Then you did do it?

71

CLITTERHOUSE

Yes.

DAISY

You never! ...

CLITTERHOUSE

(*Leans back, puts pen away*)

Well, can you make up your mind?

OAKIE

If *you* can't, I'll soon put him on to someone who can.

KELLERMAN

Where have you got the stuff?

CLITTERHOUSE

(*Pause*)

Here! (*He produces jewels from his pocket.* OAKIE *rises.*)

PAL

You said you hadn't got it.

CLITTERHOUSE

I beg your pardon. I asked if you thought I carried it about with me.... As a matter of fact, I do. (*Unwrapping wash-leather on knees.*)

OAKIE

(*Steps behind* PAL)

Stone me, you're a knockout.

KELLERMAN

Here, I'll have a look at them. (*Crosses to table in front of* DAISY, *pushing her aside. Sits in chair, behind table.*)

72

DAISY

And you back-answered the sergeant with all this on you!
(CLITTERHOUSE *puts jewels on table.* PAL *rises.*)

OAKIE

If he'd picked you up with all that on you, we'd have all
been pinched.

CLITTERHOUSE
(*Sorts it out*)
Number one job—number—try that on, Daisy! (*He passes
necklet to her.*)

DAISY

Heavy, isn't it?

CLITTERHOUSE
I'll fasten it. (*He does so.*)

OAKIE

Benny, how much is that worth? (*Moves round to* KEL-
LERMAN, *who picks up a piece of jewelry.*)

CLITTERHOUSE
Two thousand pounds, according to the original owner.

KELLERMAN
Two hundred's my price. (CLITTERHOUSE *looks at* KELLER-
MAN.)

DAISY
(*Looking in mirror on wall*)
I don't like it. . . . It's too flash!

73

PAL

Yes, Woolworth's....

CLITTERHOUSE

Inspector Charles called it a dog-collar.

KELLERMAN
(*Turns*)

Now, why keep bringing his name into it?...Has he seen it?

CLITTERHOUSE
(*Turns to* KELLERMAN)

Well, he's looking for it.... (*Loud laugh from* PAL *and* OAKIE) Well, what's it all worth—to you?

KELLERMAN

Well, I'll tell you. (*Producing watchmaker's glass.*)

OAKIE

You know! You done yourself a bit o' good with this lot. But you done too many jobs for it. (DAISY *tries necklet round waist, then round wrist, admiringly.*)

CLITTERHOUSE

You think so?

OAKIE

Yes, go after it big, in an' out quick....That's my motto.

CLITTERHOUSE

And a very good one, too. What's your line?

74

OAKIE

That all depends.

PAL

I'll tell you.... Now and again he cracks a safe, but mostly it's straight stealing.... Hot on locks, Oakie is.

DAISY

(*Drops necklet in front of* KELLERMAN)
They're on something tonight.

CLITTERHOUSE

You are?...

DAISY

Don't forget this, Benny....

OAKIE

Yes.... That's why I didn't want to talk to that copper.

DAISY

You didn't ought to do it, Oakie, not with the sergeant after you.

OAKIE

(*Laughs*)
Don't you worry. I'll look in and see him first! (PAL *laughs.*)

CLITTERHOUSE

I suppose you're an expert?

PAL

He's more'n that—he's good!

CLITTERHOUSE

Are you in this too, Pal?

OAKIE

He is.

CLITTERHOUSE

You know, we might do something together, sometime. . . .

OAKIE

(*Looks at* PAL, *who nods and winks.* OAKIE *winks at* PAL. *Turns to* CLITTERHOUSE)

I don't see why not?

CLITTERHOUSE

We'll see . . . shall we?

OAKIE

Yes!

KELLERMAN

Well, I've priced 'em. (*Puts pieces to one side.*) That for valuing.

CLITTERHOUSE

Oh, you take a rake-off for valuing, do you?

OAKIE

Yes! He'd take the whole issue, if you let him.

DAISY

Don't let him put it across you too much.

76

KELLERMAN

(*Glaring at her*)

I'll give you four hundred quid for the rest.

CLITTERHOUSE

Four hundred? But the stuff's worth five thousand!

KELLERMAN

(*Obstinately, not looking at him*)

Four hundred. . . .

CLITTERHOUSE

Oh! I mean that's taking all the profit out of crime! . . .
Make it a thousand.

OAKIE

You want to get him to price it before you do the jobs.

KELLERMAN

Shut up, Oakie. (OAKIE *says: "Oh, all right," and crosses
above table*) I don't deal in small stuff like this.

CLITTERHOUSE

No. But raise it a bit . . . I mean, a dissatisfied customer is
not much of a recommendation. (OAKIE *sits on edge of table,
lights cigarette.*)

PAL

Come on, Benny . . . be fair!

KELLERMAN

Oh! All right. Five hundred, then—and that's too much.

77

CLITTERHOUSE

All right. . . .

KELLERMAN
(*Rises*)

I'll give you the money tomorrow. (*Wrapping up jewels.*)

CLITTERHOUSE

I'll have it now.

KELLERMAN

"Well, I, er . . . I haven't got that much about me . . . I might give you a bit on account.

CLITTERHOUSE

All—or nothing, and I take the stuff away with me.

DAISY
(*Quietly*)

You've got the dough, Benny!

KELLERMAN
(*Glares at her again*)

Oh, all right. I'll see what I can find. (*Goes to door, putting jewels in pocket.*)

CLITTERHOUSE
(*Catching* KELLERMAN's *arm*)

Just a moment. (KELLERMAN *turns. He is standing beside* CLITTERHOUSE, *jewels in both hands.* CLITTERHOUSE *takes them*) Not that I don't trust you, of course. And bring back the five hundred.

KELLERMAN

If I've got it. (*Glares at* CLITTERHOUSE *and exits. All laugh.*
CLITTERHOUSE *smiles.*)

PAL

You ain't cautious, are you, mate!

DAISY

That's the way to treat Benny.... You're started right.

OAKIE

He's tight all right, but he's safe. You won't know that
stuff by the morning. (PAL *goes to slot machine.*)

CLITTERHOUSE

What will he do with it?

OAKIE

Take out the stones and melt down the settings.

DAISY

He won't. He'll pass that lot on.

CLITTERHOUSE
(*To* OAKIE)
His rates of pay are not very high, are they?

OAKIE

As I told you: you want to get him to price the stuff before
you snatch it. You see, I know what we've got coming for tonight's job if it goes all right. (PAL *works slot machine.*)

79

CLITTERHOUSE

You know, Oakie, there are some things you know more about than I do.... We might work very well together. (*Jewels in hand.*)

OAKIE

We might.

DAISY

(*Standing beside* CLITTERHOUSE, *slips arm through his*) He's not bad, is he, Oakie?

CLITTERHOUSE

We'll think about it, shall we? (KELLERMAN *returns.* PAL *puts coin in machine.*)

OAKIE

Well, I like your style, China....

KELLERMAN

(*Notes in hand*)

Here you are! Five hundred. (CLITTERHOUSE *crosses slowly to* KELLERMAN *and goes to take notes.*)

PAL

Count 'em!

DAISY

They don't need counting.

OAKIE

(*Crosses to* PAL)

They're all right. When Benny pays—he pays! And you

80

know it, Pal! (KELLERMAN *holds out hand for jewels. They then exchange simultaneously. Jewels pass on top, notes underneath,* CLITTERHOUSE *snatching notes quickly.* KELLERMAN *goes behind bar.*)

CLITTERHOUSE

Well, let's have another drink to our next deal. (*Strips off top note in payment and goes to bar.*)

KELLERMAN

Have you got one in mind?

CLITTERHOUSE
(*Turning to the others*)
The same again all around?

PAL

Pigs! (*Laughing*) Take steps to bring it to the notice of your superiors at the Yard.

OAKIE

Benny, give me another o' what I had before.... (KELLERMAN *places beer out quickly.* CLITTERHOUSE *takes beer and glass to table for* PAL.)

DAISY

Dry Martinis for me—*and my gentleman friend.*

KELLERMAN

Working fast, aren't you? ... Who is he, that's what I want to know? ... (*To* CLITTERHOUSE, *who turns on this*) Here, how long have you been on this lay?

81

DAISY

Not long, you bet! (*Handing Martini to* CLITTERHOUSE, *who passes it to* OAKIE.)

KELLERMAN

How do you know?

OAKIE

Oh, thanks. You know, you're either silly-lucky, China, or else you've got something. (PAL *is pouring beer.*)

DAISY

What *is* your name? (*Hands* CLITTERHOUSE *his own Martini.*)

CLITTERHOUSE

Anything you care to call me....

OAKIE

(*Laughs*)

Oh! Ho! You wait till you know her! (PAL *laughs with* OAKIE. *All now have glasses.* CLITTERHOUSE *raises his own.*)

CLITTERHOUSE

Well, here's to crime—and research!

KELLERMAN

And what?

CLITTERHOUSE

Oh, well, never mind—let's make it plain crime!

DAISY

Cheerio!

82

CLITTERHOUSE

Crime!

OAKIE

Looking at you, China!

PAL

Rot him! (*All laugh and drink.*)

Quick Curtain

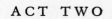

ACT TWO

ACT TWO

Scene I

SCENE: *The lounge of a ground-floor flat in Bloomsbury, in the late evening, four months later. The room is expensively furnished, equipped with a cocktail cabinet. A door, right, leads to the rest of the flat; another door, left, forms an entrance through the kitchen, from a yard and mews beyond.* PAL GREEN *is lying almost full length on a settee. His shirt-sleeve is rolled high on his left arm. Jacket on chair, with hat on top of it.* DAISY *is kneeling by his head, with tourniquet gripping the upper part of his arm. She wears a semi-evening frock.* OAKIE *is sitting on settee with* PAL's *left arm across his knee. As curtain rises he is reaching to cabinet behind him for swab, then leans forward and dabs* PAL's *arm.*

PAL
(*Lifts head*)
Here! What's the idea of this, Oakie?

OAKIE
Hold still, Pal. (*Pushes his head back. Dabs with swab, then puts it on cabinet.*)

DAISY
(*Hopefully*)
Isn't there going to be any blood?

OAKIE
Not unless he bursts when I prick him.... (PAL *sits up violently, pushes* OAKIE *away.* DAISY *lets tourniquet slip.*)

87

PAL

Here half a mo'. I've changed my mind. I'm not going to have it done! (*Sits squarely, with feet down.*)

OAKIE

Please yourself, mate....

PAL

I can't see what he wants it for!

DAISY

All right, you can tell him so when he comes....

PAL

He's always mucking about....

OAKIE

Now look here! Are you going to let me do this, or aren't you?

PAL

Will it hurt?

OAKIE

No....I done mine meself.

PAL

What's it for?

DAISY

He says it's a blood test.

PAL

Blood test! My blood's red, the same as anybody else's....

DAISY

It isn't, it's blue....

OAKIE

Blue?

DAISY

That's what he says.... It's blue inside you, and it comes out red.

PAL

Well, that's a bloody lie to start with.

OAKIE

(*Crosses back to settee*)

Oh! Shut your face and lay down.... (*Pushing him back quickly on settee with hand on* PAL's *head. Sits on settee again, takes* PAL's *arm across his knee again*) ... Now, then, press his arm, Daisy.

DAISY

(*Adjusts the rubber tourniquet*)

Okay.

PAL

(*Raising forearm*)

How much are you going to draw off?

OAKIE

(*Jerks arm down*)

Hold still, Pal.... Now then.... Clench your fist a couple of times. (PAL *does so.*)

89

DAISY

It's all right, Pal.

OAKIE

Hold hard, mate. (*Venule goes into vein just above bend of inside arm.*)

PAL

Urch!...I felt that needle. (*Head falls back. Raises one leg.*)

OAKIE

Let go, Daisy!

DAISY

All right! (*She loosens tourniquet. But keeps it on arm. A silence.*)

PAL

Here! I'll give you a bit o' news. I don't like this. (*He brings head well up.*)

OAKIE

Oh! Shut up! (DAISY *pushes* PAL's *head down, her eyes still fixed on his arm. A pause.*)

PAL

Ain't you got enough yet? (*Another silence*) How goes it now?

DAISY

It's all right.

90

PAL

It ain't all right.... He's had time to get a gallon! Here, come on, I'm getting up.

OAKIE

Okay, mate! (*Withdraws venule. Puts swab on cabinet.* DAISY *takes tourniquet off, then rises*) Look! There's hardly a mark on your arm! (*Raises ampoule, looking through it*) Look, Daisy! Alas, my poor brother! (PAL *sits up and examines his arm, putting on eye-glasses.*)

PAL

Here! Show us how much you took.... (OAKIE *shows the ampoule, corks bottle, crosses to desk*) Blimey! Is that all? I thought you was bleeding me white. (*Takes off eye-glasses.* OAKIE *sits at desk. Commences to label ampoules.*)

DAISY

There you are, Pal. There was nothing to it.

PAL

Well, it's made me feel funny, anyway. Here, what about a bracer, Daise? (DAISY *puts cushions straight on settee.*)

OAKIE

Nothing doing.... You know his orders.

PAL

(*Fastens cuff*)

Oh! Come on, open it up, Daise. (*Gestures to cocktail cabinet.*)

DAISY

(*Behind settee*)

After the big job.

PAL

Oh! Well, I don't like being mucked about every time we do a job! Anybody'd think we was 'orspital cases. (*Puts hat on.*)

DAISY

(*Putting stopper in ether bottle*)
He never hurts you!

PAL

(*Picks up coat from chair*)
Don't he? After that Hatton Garden do, he climbed halfway down my throat!

DAISY

That was because you keep losing your voice.

OAKIE

You know very well you nearly lost it that night. . . .

PAL

(*Pulling on his coat*)
Yes, he climbed in to look for it here. If I can't get a drink here, I'm going out after one.

DAISY

He'll rumble you. . . .

PAL

Well! Let him rumble. . . .

OAKIE

Oh, all right. Oi! Look out for Tug in the yard.

PAL
(*At door*)

All right.

DAISY

And don't be long. The guv'nor'll be here soon.

PAL

I'll make it a quick one.... (PAL *exits.* DAISY *goes to cabinet and takes ether bottle.* OAKIE *has now put labels on ampoules and holds one up.*)

OAKIE
(*Looking through it*)

Neat, aren't they?... Pal's blood! My blood! (*Slips it in box.*)

DAISY

What does he want them for?

OAKIE

Research, he says.... (*Holds up other, then puts it in box*) Well, they're all ready for him.... (*Puts ampoule box on desk, crosses to cabinet for cigar.*)

DAISY
(*Sits on desk, feet on chair at desk*)

He did the same before that smash and grab.

OAKIE
(*Bites end of cigar and spits it out*)

That's right. The time Pal socked that copper—and lost his voice when he thought he'd done him in!

DAISY

Funny the way Pal's voice goes...

OAKIE

Yes! It's only when he's got excited, or gets the wind up.... Funny, the way the guv'nor keeps an eye on him. (*Lighting cigar.*)

DAISY

He makes more fuss over Pal than he does over me. (OAKIE *throws match down*) Here! Mind the carpet. (DAISY *crosses, picks up match.*)

OAKIE

You got a lot to grumble about, I must say.... He fitted you up with all this, didn't he?

DAISY

(*Crossing below settee to mantel*)

Yes! But he never stops here.... What good's that? (*Puts match in ashtray.*)

OAKIE

Here, Daisy. You're not going to tell me he hasn't ever... *You know!*

DAISY

If you only knew how I've tried.... If I do start anything, he sort of slips away.... You know, he's matey, but none o' that there! (*Slight pause.*)

OAKIE

Oh! Well, what's it matter?

94

DAISY

(*Facing him*)

If he'd only let himself go a bit, I might find something out.

OAKIE

You don't want to worry.... He's the best crook I've ever met.

DAISY

Still, I'd like to know.

OAKIE

(*Confidentially*)

D'you know what I think? I think he's been a medical bloke wot's got in bad.

DAISY

And mucking about like this keeps his hand in, eh?

OAKIE

That's right. It's a sort of an 'obby, I expect.

DAISY

He always phones somebody before he goes. I wish I knew who it was.... I don't even know what the number is.

OAKIE

Oh, well. You take him as he comes.

DAISY

I got to....

OAKIE

He's a damn fine crook.... Look what he's pulled off. Benny told me that tonight's job was big enough to frighten even him.

95

(*There is a ring at the front doorbell. Two or three short rings, which* DAISY *recognizes.*)

DAISY

That's him! (DAISY *rises, goes quickly to the door and exits, leaving door open. During pause,* OAKIE *helps himself to two or three cigars*) Hello, dear! (*Off stage.*)

CLITTERHOUSE
(*Off stage*)

Hello, Daisy.... How are you? (*Enters, carrying bag*) Hello, Oakie!

OAKIE
(*Rises*)

Watcher, China.... I done 'em.... Pal's is still warm. (DAISY *re-enters, closes door.*)

CLITTERHOUSE

Good man! ... Have you the boxes there?

OAKIE

Yes! Over here. (OAKIE *crosses to desk.*)

CLITTERHOUSE

Where is Pal?

DAISY

He'll be back in a minute.

CLITTERHOUSE
(*Hands bag to* DAISY)

Good. (*She puts it on desk. She knows* PAL *has gone for a*

96

drink) I've brought something for his throat. (*Crosses to fireplace*) When's Kellerman coming?

OAKIE

(*Putting tops on ampoule boxes*)
He ought to be here any minute now....

CLITTERHOUSE

Well, Oakie! (*Produces cigarette case.* DAISY *takes matches from cabinet, crosses to* CLITTERHOUSE) Do you feel ready for it?

OAKIE

Yes, I got it all taped....

CLITTERHOUSE

Did you do what I told you last night?

OAKIE

Yes. (DAISY *solicitously lights* CLITTERHOUSE's *cigarette, then goes to mantel.*)

OAKIE

It was a push-over.... I can pick that lock again any time.

CLITTERHOUSE

Good! How long did it take?

OAKIE

Under a minute.... It was dead easy!

CLITTERHOUSE

Oakie, this is going to be a very neat job.

97

DAISY
(*Crosses to him and sits on back of settee*)
They always are when you do them.

CLITTERHOUSE
(*Takes her hand in his*)
And you're going to have a nice fur coat out of it.

DAISY

Honest?

CLITTERHOUSE
Yes, mink. It's just a little present, Daisy.

DAISY
It's ever so nice of you. (*She puts arms round his neck, but he rises and goes to desk for ampoule boxes.*)

CLITTERHOUSE
I went down to the warehouse this afternoon to pick out the skins. You'll have to go to the furriers to choose the style of coat you want.

DAISY
Aren't you thieving it?

CLITTERHOUSE
(*Turns, ampoules in hand*)
Good heavens, no! Besides, there are no made-up furs in the warehouse.

OAKIE
Guv'nor, do you mean to say you picked the furs there?
98

CLITTERHOUSE

I made that an excuse to go along this afternoon.

OAKIE

(*Amazed*)

You've been on the job—today!

CLITTERHOUSE

(*Puts ampoules in bag and closes it*)

I thought it might be as well to make sure that everything is in proper order for tonight.... (*A door slams*) Would that be Pal?

DAISY

It ought to be.... (PAL *enters by the kitchen door with* "TUG" WILSON—*a burly, moustached man.*)

PAL

(*Comes in quickly.* TUG *is at his right*)

Hello, Guv'nor.... (*Stops short, puts hand over mouth, backs away*) I met Tug outside.

CLITTERHOUSE

(*Shakes* TUG's *hand*)

Good evening, Tug.... How are you?

TUG

(*Coming forward, grinning*)

All right, cully.... Here, you're not going to do any o' that funny stuff with me, are you? ... I had me tonsils out when I was a nipper. (TUG *keeps hat on all through scene.*)

CLITTERHOUSE

All you've got to do is to drive the lorry. Where's your mate —what's his name?—Sammy?

99

TUG

Aw!! I wouldn't bring him up *here!*

OAKIE

I've told him what he's got to do.

CLITTERHOUSE
(*To* TUG)

Have you been over it with him?

TUG

He's got to empty the sacks into the boxes and help me load 'em on the lorry.

CLITTERHOUSE

That's it. Oakie, what about "Badger" Lee?

OAKIE

He'll be along presently.

CLITTERHOUSE

He'll come on the roof with us....

OAKIE

Yes. I wouldn't trust him down below.

CLITTERHOUSE

No.... Now, I want to go over it once more and ... (*Someone blunders against the kitchen door.* "BADGER" LEE *enters. He slips in and closes the door behind him.*)

OAKIE

Watcher, Badger.

100

BADGER

Hello! ... Hello, Daise. (*Takes cap off, comes slowly round cabinet.* Evening, Guv'nor. (*To* CLITTERHOUSE.)

CLITTERHOUSE
(*Rises*)

How are you, Badger?

BADGER

Oh, I'm all right.

CLITTERHOUSE

Tell me, tonight's not going to be too much for you?

PAL

(*Coming to front of settee, behind* CLITTERHOUSE)

Badger's a good 'un, Guv'nor.... He's a bit nervous because o' the times wot he's been jugged.

TUG

All right. 'Ave it yer own way, Cully.

CLITTERHOUSE

I wish you wouldn't call me Cully.

TUG

What the 'ell can I call you? You ain't got a name.

PAL

You can talk. You never had your blood took off in a bottle ... and it wasn't blue neither!

OAKIE

It is blue, but it comes out red.

CLITTERHOUSE

All right! *All right!!*

PAL

You can't kid me. I bleed red, I do!

CLITTERHOUSE

(*Turns, frowns at* PAL, *and sits on arm of settee*)

Now, let's get through this before Kellerman comes. You know where to plant your lorry, Tug?

TUG

I do.

CLITTERHOUSE

What do you do, Pal?

PAL

(*Looking up, as if reciting*)

I wait at the front o' the place, until I see the watchman register on the bottom clock.

CLITTERHOUSE

That's right. Then you walk down to the corner and round into the street....

PAL

Right!

OAKIE

As soon as I see Pal come into the street, I go for the door and start on the lock.

CLITTERHOUSE

You've got it pat! ... Now, while Oakie works on the lock, I come down from the other end of the street. Pal and I meet at the door just after Oakie has opened it. (*We assume* CLITTER-HOUSE *can smell beer on* PAL's *breath. So* PAL *must come in close.*)

BADGER

I can do with a right job, just now.... My cut's three hundred, ain't it? (PAL *is behind* CLITTERHOUSE *now.*)

CLITTERHOUSE

Three hundred it is, Badger. (*Turns to* PAL, *whose face is near his shoulder.*) Pal, didn't Oakie tell you to keep off it until afterwards?

PAL

I only had a quick one, Guv.

OAKIE

(*Steps in close behind* CLITTERHOUSE)
Yes, it kind o' turned him up when I drew that blood off him.

PAL

Honest, it did.... I thought I was going to pass out.

DAISY

He needed a bracer....

CLITTERHOUSE

Well, I suppose that excuses you. (CLITTERHOUSE *moves toward* TUG) Now, Tug—

TUG

I ain't touched nothing. Want to smell my breath?

CLITTERHOUSE

No, thank you. I'll postpone that pleasure till later.

PAL

One I had, that's all.

OAKIE

One's enough, mate.

PAL

Think he's wild with me?

DAISY

We told you not to go.

OAKIE

What about Nobbler?

CLITTERHOUSE

He'll follow me.

PAL

Oh! S'truth!! What we got to have Nobbler for?

OAKIE

Oh! Somebody's got to pick the best furs, you fool!

CLITTERHOUSE

He knows just what's on the racks and rails, and he'll load the sacks for us.

TUG

(*Stepping in*)

Can't *you* pick the stuff?

CLITTERHOUSE

Oh, my dear fellow. I don't know the difference between a Russian sable and an imitation mink. Nobbler is an expert!

OAKIE

He'll earn his cut, mate.

TUG

Oh, all right.

BADGER

Here, I got to wait after you've gone in, ain't I?

CLITTERHOUSE

Do you know how long you wait?

BADGER

Seven minutes.

OAKIE

Have you got a ticker?

BADGER

Yes! Here you are.... (*Produces watch from trousers' pocket.*)

CLITTERHOUSE

You'll come right up to the top floor, and wait with Nobbler.

BADGER

(*Steps in*)

Who's going to work that little lift what sends the sacks down?

PAL

My brother, Bert.

CLITTERHOUSE

Pal's brother, Bert. (*Imitating* PAL'S *accent.*)

BADGER

Me and 'im comes in together....

PAL

Yes. I'm with the empty sacks.

CLITTERHOUSE

Right. Oakie, after we come in with Pal, we go up to the roof, and climb over on to that lead flat I told you about. You remember?

PAL

(*Reciting*)

We opens the warehouse skylight, and goes down to the second floor.

OAKIE

And meet the watchman.

CLITTERHOUSE

Right! (*Rises, goes to* TUG) Now then.... You be the watchman. Come over here. (*He takes* TUG *by the arm and leads him*

106

to the left, where he stays) You're coming up the stairs.... It's quite dark, remember. (CLITTERHOUSE *switches out lights.*) Oakie, this is the first partition here, and I let him come by me.... (OAKIE *crosses to above desk*) Pal, you're there. That's round the angle of the wall.... (PAL *crosses, stands below cabinet*) No, Oakie, you're there, in the doorway I told you about. Remember? (OAKIE *moves below chair at desk.*)

OAKIE

I get you. (PAL *and* OAKIE *stand and button up their coats for action.* CLITTERHOUSE *is behind the settee.*)

CLITTERHOUSE

I let the watchman go by me. Now, walk forward, Tug. (*He comes up to* PAL *and* OAKIE. TUG *passes him*) That's right. (TUG *turns left of cabinet*) Now, as he draws level ... Grab him! (OAKIE *puts wristlock on* TUG. PAL *grabs his left arm.* CLITTERHOUSE *puts handkerchief over his face from behind.* TUG *gurgles*) You two keep that hold on him. Stand away from his legs in case he kicks. Count ten from the moment I get my mask over his mouth and nose. (*Lowering* TUG *slowly on to his back*) And the watchman comes gently to the ground. (CLITTERHOUSE *switches on the lights.*)

OAKIE

It's a gift. (*Both shake hands. All laughing.* PAL *crosses to cabinet.* OAKIE *to right.* TUG *rises, crosses to* DAISY. PAL *slaps him on back as he passes.*)

CLITTERHOUSE

(*Moving behind settee and sits on its arm*)

I shall have to give the watchman a little attention, once he's down, but that won't take long.

BADGER

He won't pass out, will he?

CLITTERHOUSE

Good heavens, no. . . . I've done too many of them!

PAL
(*Steps in*)
Watchmen? (*Then half sits on cabinet*)

CLITTERHOUSE
(*Behind settee*)
Well, not watchmen exactly. Now, don't forget, we all put on gloves the moment we're inside the factory. . . . Especially you, Badger.

BADGER

Yes, Guv'nor. . . .

TUG

They got too many of his prints at the Yard already. (*Laughs.* CLITTERHOUSE *stares at him. He turns away.*)

CLITTERHOUSE

Daisy has gloves for everyone.

DAISY

They're in there. Come on, Badger. (*Crosses to cabinet*) Out of the light, Pal. (BADGER, *following* DAISY, *goes past* PAL.)

OAKIE
(*Comes to* PAL)
We might as well all take them now. (DAISY *gives gloves in rubber band to* PAL, *who gives pair to* OAKIE *and* BADGER.)

TUG

This is where I come into the picture ain't it, Guv'nor?

CLITTERHOUSE

That's right, Tug. You bring your lorry outside Bellman's box factory at exactly twenty minutes to one.

OAKIE

And don't forget that your mate puts the light on in the factory.

DAISY

(*Gives loose gloves to* TUG)

So's you look like you've got a right to be there. (*Then in an aside*) These are for Sammy.

CLITTERHOUSE

That's most essential. Now, there's just one thing that may crop up.... The policeman.

BADGER

(*Alarmed*)

What one?

CLITTERHOUSE

The one on the beat outside the box factory.

BADGER

Oh! I don't like the sound o' that!

PAL

Ssh! It'll be all right, mate. (*This is an aside.*)

TUG

Me and my mate have got all that taped, Guv'nor.... We got the lorry dolled up with the same name as the box factory. Bellmans. My yarn is that them boxes have got to go to Aldgate to be packed.... It's a rush job.

CLITTERHOUSE
(*Coming round to front of settee*)
That's right. And you grumble because you have to be up all night taking them to the docks. Now that's your story, if the policeman does comes along.

OAKIE
Do you know which docks, Tug?

TUG
West India docks. Here! Suppose the copper's suspicious?

CLITTERHOUSE
Well, if I'm not there already, I'll come down then.

PAL
And choke 'im off like you did Sergeant Horace!

CLITTERHOUSE
Something like that.

OAKIE
The beauty of it is we pinch the furs from a warehouse in one street—

PAL
And load it up out of a factory what makes empty boxes in another.

OAKIE

It's a natural. (*Laughing. Shakes hands with* PAL.)

TUG

And when do we cut it up?

CLITTERHOUSE

Here, tomorrow night . . . at nine o'clock.

OAKIE

And we start the ball rolling at half past eleven tonight.

CLITTERHOUSE

Yes. Well, I think that's all for the present. . . . You can get along, Tug, and you too, Badger. . . . Just keep your heads, and everything will go all right.

BADGER

(*Steps down*)

Have you got a minder over that copper?

CLITTERHOUSE

We don't need one. . . .

BADGER

Daise could look out for him.

DAISY

(*Eagerly*)

I've done it before. . . . I'll come!

CLITTERHOUSE

There's no necessity, Daisy. We can deal with the policeman when he turns up. (DAISY *is disappointed*.)

III

BADGER

Well, do we get a drink to wet the job now? (PAL *looks expectant.*)

CLITTERHOUSE

No. You heard what I said to Pal. (PAL *scowls*) And don't come near this place until tomorrow night.

TUG

(*Opens door*)
Come on, Badger.... Twenty to one!...I'll be there.

BADGER

So long.... (*Exit* BADGER.)

CLITTERHOUSE

Good-bye....

OAKIE

And don't go near any boozers.

TUG

(*Grinning*)
I'll see he don't.... (*Exit* TUG, *closing door.* PAL *straddles chair at desk.*)

CLITTERHOUSE

You know, I don't think Badger is too safe....

OAKIE

We can look after him.

CLITTERHOUSE

His heart is bad ... and his nerves are all shot to pieces.

112

OAKIE

Yes, he'll drink himself nuts with his cut. . . . Three hundred quid's a lot to him.

CLITTERHOUSE

So long as he doesn't start talking.

PAL

No. Badger don't never say nothing. . . .

CLITTERHOUSE

You didn't say much yourself just then.

OAKIE

He don't chatter!

DAISY

(*Coming to settee, sits beside* CLITTERHOUSE)
Well, for God's sake, don't *you* get lagged.

PAL

(*Frightened*)
Here, Daise! Don't start talking like that, Daise. . . . It's unlucky.

CLITTERHOUSE

(*Leaning back*)
I wonder what my friend, Inspector Charles, of Scotland Yard, would say to all this. You know—I've often discussed our activities with him. . . . And he says that a well-organized gang of international crooks had been at work. . . . Note the well-organized. . . . I can remember the time when he had a very different opinion.

113

PAL

Note the international!

OAKIE

Blimey!!

DAISY

You're doing this very clever....

CLITTERHOUSE

Aren't we, Daisy? It should be all over inside two hours. (*There is a ring on the bell.*)

OAKIE

Hello, that'll be Benny. (DAISY *exits.*) What's he going to pay, Guv'nor?

CLITTERHOUSE

I don't know ... but I know the approximate value of the furs.

PAL

Don't let him take any rake-off!

CLITTERHOUSE

I certainly won't. (*Turns.* KELLERMAN *enters*) Good evening, Mr. Kellerman.

KELLERMAN

Evening. (DAISY *re-enters*) Evening, all.... Got a drink, Daise? (*Sits, looking very grim.*)

DAISY

What'll you have?

114

KELLERMAN

Whisky straight. (DAISY *takes out bottle and glass*.)

CLITTERHOUSE

You look a little off color, Mr. Kellerman.

KELLERMAN

This job worries me....

OAKIE

Why? Been to the warehouse?

KELLERMAN

I went there yesterday....

DAISY

Anything for anybody else?

CLITTERHOUSE

Nothing for anybody else, Daisy, except **you.** (**KELLERMAN**
looks at CLITTERHOUSE.)

DAISY

I won't drink without you.... (KELLERMAN *looks at* DAISY
and holds the look.)

CLITTERHOUSE

Well! That's very charming of you.... But you must excuse
me....

OAKIE

Come on, Benny. How much do you make it? (CLITTERHOUSE
turns and takes cigarette from mantel.)

KELLERMAN
(*Still looking at* DAISY)
I'll tell you in a minute.... (*Picks up glass from cabinet*)
Luck to all. (*Very grudgingly, and drinks.*)

PAL
We can use it....

KELLERMAN
I felt funny, I give you my word, when I was in there.

CLITTERHOUSE
All eyes, aren't they? (*Lights cigarette.*)

KELLERMAN
They know they've got something worth thieving.... I took
a good look at it, though.

PAL
I hope you got an eyeful....

KELLERMAN
I did. But ... (*Finishes drink*) I'm still in two minds about
going on with the job.

CLITTERHOUSE
Why is that?

OAKIE
Here. You're not backing out, are you?

KELLERMAN
The cops will be up there like a swarm of bees tomorrow.
116

CLITTERHOUSE

Well, they won't find anything....

KELLERMAN

Won't they? Tug's on the lorry.... Supposing he's seen—
and traced to me!

CLITTERHOUSE

Tug's let his moustache grow for this job—so has Sammy....
They won't be recognized.

KELLERMAN

I hope not. Well, if this comes off, it'll be one of the fattest
swipes that's ever been done in furs.

OAKIE

(*Growling*)

What d'you mean—if!

DAISY

Nothing's ever gone wrong before!

KELLERMAN

Once is enough!... But it ought to be all right. (*Looks at*
CLITTERHOUSE) I've got my end fixed.

CLITTERHOUSE

I went over the ground today. I was telling Daisy that I
picked out the skins for her new fur coat.

KELLERMAN

I can buy her all the fur coats she wants.

117

DAISY

I don't—the guv'nor's got taste.... (OAKIE *nudges* PAL. *Both giggle*) You needn't bother. (*Goes to* CLITTERHOUSE, *showing her frock*) Bought me this, he did....

CLITTERHOUSE

Pretty, isn't it?

KELLERMAN

Not bad.... Where'd you thieve it?

CLITTERHOUSE

Thieve it! My dear Mr. Kellerman—I bought it!

OAKIE

Come on, Benny, what about pricing this stuff?

PAL

Yes!

KELLERMAN

Well, you want cash, don't you?

CLITTERHOUSE
(*Briskly*)

One-pound notes...here...tomorrow night. Nine o'clock.

OAKIE

And no snide notes nor sticky ones, neither.

KELLERMAN

Well, I know I can dispose of the stuff, and I've arranged all that.... My price—and it's the limit—is fourteen thousand....

118

PAL

Gaw! Blimey!

DAISY

Oh! Er!

OAKIE

That's talking, Benny!

CLITTERHOUSE
(*Steps in*)
That's a thousand short of my figure.

KELLERMAN

I couldn't give any more if I wanted to. I've had the hell of a job collecting the dough.

CLITTERHOUSE

All right, let it go at that.... Fourteen thousand. (*Turns away to mantel, puts out cigarette.*)

DAISY

Are you shifting it quick?

KELLERMAN

So quick, I'll hardly see it.... I'll be glad when this is all over.... I give you my word.

DAISY

So shall I....

CLITTERHOUSE
(*Turns, smiling*)
I'm rather looking forward to it.

119

KELLERMAN

You would. Are you still doing that medical stuff o' yours?

OAKIE

(*Pointing to bag on desk*)

Yes! He's got two bottles of blood in that bag.

PAL

(*Boasting*)

Yes, my blood.

OAKIE

Eh?

PAL

And Oakie's.

KELLERMAN

I don't get that side of you. . . .

CLITTERHOUSE

Well, don't let it worry you. Well, I'll meet you two tonight at eleven-thirty as arranged. (*Sits at desk.* KELLERMAN *makes a sign to* DAISY, *who crosses to* CLITTERHOUSE *to see number he will dial.*)

OAKIE

(*Sitting in armchair*)

We'll be there, Guv'nor! (CLITTERHOUSE *dials twice, then turns, smiles at* DAISY *and turns phone.* DAISY *gestures to* KELLERMAN *and leans against door.*)

CLITTERHOUSE

(*Dialing at telephone*)

Talking about time, Oakie, you won't forget to work the watchman's clocks, will you?

OAKIE

Every quarter of an hour....

CLITTERHOUSE

And in the proper order....

OAKIE

I won't forget.

CLITTERHOUSE

Well, the alarm will go off if you do.

KELLERMAN

(*Sarcastically*)

I suppose you've got everything else fixed?

CLITTERHOUSE

(*Half turns to him*)

Oh! Nicely fixed, thank you. Hello.... Yes, it is.... Yes, I shall be there in about twenty minutes, but I shall be back rather late tonight, I'm afraid.... I beg your pardon? ... Oh, he's there now.... Well, put him on to me, will you? (*Covers mouthpiece. Rises. Sits on edge of desk*) I've got a friend of yours on the other end of the wire, Mister Kellerman.

KELLERMAN

Who is it?

CLITTERHOUSE

You'll hear in a moment.... Well, if it isn't my old friend Inspector Charles of Scotland Yard! (DAISY *steps away from door*. KELLERMAN *rises*. OAKIE *sits up in chair*.)

PAL

Love old Ireland!

CLITTERHOUSE

What are you doing down my way? Still showing willing on
Lady Challing's burglary? Me? I'm up in Town.... I've got
rather an important engagement, I'm afraid.... Well, I must
admit there is a lady in it. (*Smiling,* DAISY *goes to* CLITTER-
HOUSE. *He puts his arm round her*) Oh, quite beautiful....
(DAISY *and* KELLERMAN *react to this*) All right, old man, sorry
to have missed you. See you soon. Good-bye. (*Hangs up.*)

KELLERMAN

Were you bluffing?

CLITTERHOUSE

No, Mister Kellerman.... You looked startled, Pal....

PAL
(*Very hoarsely*)
It give me a turn ... you talking to that busy!

CLITTERHOUSE
(*Eagerly*)
Hello, is your voice going again? This is a bit of luck—
(*Crosses to him*) I've wanted to catch you like this.... Oakie,
bring that lamp over.... Sit on the settee, Pal. (*Leads* PAL *to
settee*) Daisy, give me my bag. (DAISY *crosses quickly to desk.
Both sit. To* KELLERMAN) Bring that over. (OAKIE *brings lamp
from behind settee.* KELLERMAN *puts pouffe at* CLITTERHOUSE'S
feet, then crosses to front of cabinet. DAISY *opens bag in crossing
and puts it on pouffe.*)

122

KELLERMAN

What's the idea?

CLITTERHOUSE

He's got a laryngeal spasm.

DAISY

No! He means his voice has gone again.... (*Crosses front of* KELLERMAN. *Sits next to* PAL. CLITTERHOUSE *takes head mirror from bag and puts it on.*)

CLITTERHOUSE

No, no, Oakie, put that lamp to one side—I want to reflect the light. (OAKIE *puts lamp behind* PAL. CLITTERHOUSE *reaches for spatula and laryngeal mirror, then turns down head mirror, which makes* PAL *jerk back.*)

DAISY

I'll hold his head. (*She does so, and* CLITTERHOUSE *puts spatula in* PAL'S *mouth.*)

OAKIE

It's Okay, Pal. He's going down after your voice again ... got tools this time.

CLITTERHOUSE

That's it.... Now then.... (*Comes forward with laryngeal mirror. During this activity, the*

Curtain falls quickly

ACT TWO

Scene II

SCENE: *On a roof near Upper Thames Street, London, at 12:30 A.M., the same night.*

A lead flat, above the premises of a warehouse, is cut off by low railings from another flat on the roof of a box manufacturer. On the right of the first flat is a trap-door. Exit from the other flat is provided by a small door under a sloping roof. Upstage of this, the railings form a bay, and it is possible for anyone on the roof to look over the rail and see the street below. As the curtain rises CLITTERHOUSE *is sitting on the center railing. There is one sack lying on the left of this rail and* PAL *is crossing from the door for it.* BADGER *is taking a sack from* OAKIE, *who is inside the trap-door.* BADGER *brings sacks.* PAL *takes them from him at the rail and throws them down the trap-door. The action is smooth and rhythmic—not hurried. The fourth sack, which* BADGER *takes from* OAKIE, *has furs hanging out of it. All work and speak under nervous tension, but quietly and without any great haste. They cross and re-cross three times with sacks, before* BADGER *speaks.*

BADGER

(*Putting it over rail*)

There's some furs falling out of that one. (*Goes back to* OAKIE *for another.*)

PAL

(*Taking sack*)

All right, I'll shove 'em back. (*Crosses left.*)

124

CLITTERHOUSE

(*Looking at watch*)

We're doing very well—five minutes ahead of my programme. (BADGER *puts sack over rail.* PAL *takes it.* BADGER *pauses at rail. Wipes forehead.*)

OAKIE

(*Sack on ledge*)

Been on it about an hour, haven't we, Guv'nor?

CLITTERHOUSE

(*Crosses* BADGER *to* OAKIE)

Just an hour. Where are you now?

OAKIE

Just clearing the third floor. You know, them white ones. (BADGER *takes sack from ledge to rail.* PAL *takes it and listens at trap-door.*)

CLITTERHOUSE

I know—Arctic fox? Oakie, punch the second floor clock when you go down this time. (BADGER *slowly lifts heavy sack, which* OAKIE *has left near trap.*)

OAKIE

Right-oh, Guv'nor! (*He disappears.*)

PAL

(*To* BERT *below*)

Comin' down, Bert...eh?...(*Listens a moment*) My brother Bert wants to know if he can knock off for a pint o' beer.

CLITTERHOUSE

If he knows where to get one at this time of night, I should feel inclined to join him.

PAL

Likes his beer, Bert does ... 'ere, Guv'nor ... Ain't it about time Tug turned up with that lorry?.

CLITTERHOUSE
(*Looks at watch*)

He's due now....

BADGER
(*Dragging sack from trap-door*)

They're getting a bit heavy, Guv'nor....

CLITTERHOUSE

Here, let me help you! (*Crosses behind* BADGER *and helps sack over. As* PAL *takes sack, the sound of a motor is heard off left.*)

PAL
(*Listening*)

That sounds like the lorry! (*Drops sack and goes on rostrum. Looking down to front of building*) It's him! (BADGER *crosses to trap. Waits for more sacks.*)

CLITTERHOUSE
(*Looks at watch*)

He's dead on time! (*The motor stops.*)

PAL

Thank Gawd for that.... We'd be sunk if he hadn't turned up.

126

CLITTERHOUSE
(*To* PAL)
Take that, then nip below.... Badger, get over the railings and take the others from me. (PAL *exits.* BADGER *over rail.* OAKIE *appears with two sacks of white furs.*)

OAKIE
Another Arctic fox, Guv'nor.... (*Heaves the sack out, then drags up another.*)

CLITTERHOUSE
Tug's just arrived.

OAKIE
(*With second sack*)
Good! Has he brought any beer with him?

CLITTERHOUSE
(*Taking sacks*)
If he had, it wouldn't get past brother Bert.... Did you punch that clock? (*Crossing with sacks. Leaves them near rail.*)

OAKIE
Good and proper, Guv'nor.... (OAKIE *disappears.* CLITTERHOUSE *climbs over rail and goes to rostrum and looks down to the street.* BADGER *takes one sack to the door. Leaves it there and goes back to rail for another.*)

CLITTERHOUSE
(*On rostrum*)
Tug's quick! He's got one on the lorry already.

BADGER
(*At rail for other sack*)
Any sign o' that copper, Guv'nor?

CLITTERHOUSE
No ... but he's almost certain to come along.

BADGER
I hope he don't.... (*Pitches first sack through door*) ...
Heads up, Bert. (*Loudly.* CLITTERHOUSE *says: "Sh!"*) And
again! (*More softly, throwing other down, and crossing to
rail*) Hot, ain't it, Guv'nor? ... Sort of close.

CLITTERHOUSE
(*Watching street*)
I thought it was chilly.... Tug's working like a beaver down
there!

BADGER
(*Over rail*)
He's a good bloke! (OAKIE *reappears with two sacks.* BADGER
takes them.)

OAKIE
Nobbler's just starting on the fourth floor.... We'll be
wanting empties again in a minute.

CLITTERHOUSE
(*Coming to rail*)
All right.... (OAKIE *disappears*) Badger! Put those over the
railings. (BADGER *takes one to* CLITTERHOUSE. *He goes to door
with sack, throws it down and calls quietly.* BADGER *brings
second sack to rail. Lifts it slowly*) Bert! ... Tell them down

below that we want some more empty sacks.... (BADGER *faints.
Lets sack drop over rail. Seeing* BADGER) Here, what the...
(*Over rail to* BADGER. CLITTERHOUSE *tears open* BADGER's *collar,
listens to his heart, then stands up*) Good Lord! (*Looking
round he sees cistern. Lifts lid to see if it contains water. Soaks
handkerchief, bathes* BADGER's *head.* OAKIE *comes out of the
trap-door, dragging a sack.*)

OAKIE
Hello! What's happened? (*Puts sack on ledge.*)

CLITTERHOUSE
(*Working on him*)
Badger's fainted.... He'll be all right.... Carry on.

OAKIE
It takes him this way sometimes. (*Starting to climb out of
trap.*)

CLITTERHOUSE
You go on getting the stuff up! (OAKIE *disappears. Pause.
Empty sacks are tossed through the door on to the other flat.*
PAL *appears.*)

PAL
It's all Sir Garnet below, Guv'nor. (*Picking up empties.*)

CLITTERHOUSE
(*Stands up*)
It isn't all right here!... Badger's fainted.... You keep
things going!

PAL
(*Over rail*)
What! Is he bad?

CLITTERHOUSE
(*Throws wet handkerchief down*)
No. . . . He ought not to have been on this job.

PAL
I bet he felt that comin' on an' wouldn't say nothing. . . .
That's like him! (*Puts empty sacks on ledge.* OAKIE *reappears
with one sack and* PAL *takes it.* BADGER *stirs.* CLITTERHOUSE *kneels
by him.*)

OAKIE
How is he now?

CLITTERHOUSE
Coming round. . . .

PAL
He'll be all right.

OAKIE
How're they doing downstairs?

PAL
Workin' like hell. (*To rail with sacks.* OAKIE *takes empties
from ledge when he goes.*)

CLITTERHOUSE
(*To* BADGER)
You're all right, old chap. . . . Pal, give me one of those. . . .
Rest against this, Badger, and keep quiet for a bit. . . . (PAL
passes sack to CLITTERHOUSE *who puts it under* BADGER'S *head.*)

130

BADGER

I'm sorry, Guv'nor....

Spoken Simultaneously

CLITTERHOUSE

You couldn't help it....

PAL
(*Speaking through door*)
Bert ... Badger's heart's conked out, (*Then over rail*) but
he'll be better in a minute.

BADGER

I'm sorry, Guv'nor!

CLITTERHOUSE
(*Rises*)
You couldn't help it. You'll be better in a few minutes. (*Puts
handkerchief in pocket.*)

BADGER

I didn't let you down willingly, Guv'nor.... (*Tries to
get up.*)

CLITTERHOUSE

Stay where you are!

BADGER
(*Up on elbow*)
I'm all right now!

CLITTERHOUSE

Keep quiet, you fool! (*Lays him down again*) Badger, you
must rest there for a bit.

BADGER

Be with you in a minute.

OAKIE

(*Reappearing with two sacks*)

Is he getting over it? (PAL *takes one sack and crosses.*)

CLITTERHOUSE

(*Going to* OAKIE)

Is there a mug or something down there, so that I can give him a drink? (OAKIE *does not reply, goes after a second or two.* CLITTERHOUSE *picks up sack.*)

PAL

(*Getting over rail*)

You don't touch water, do you, Badger?

BADGER

(*On elbow, shakily*)

Only when I wash, mate.

CLITTERHOUSE

Keep quiet, Badger.

BADGER

I'm letting you down, Guv'nor.... (*Getting up slowly.*)

CLITTERHOUSE

No, you're not.... These sacks are enough to tire anybody. (*Putting sack over rail, steps back.*)

BADGER

No good to you, I'm not. (*Hanging on to rail.*)

132

PAL
(Picks up sack at rail)
Cheer up, mate . . . you'll get your cut just the same, won't he, Guv'nor?

CLITTERHOUSE
Of course he will.

BADGER
I ain't thinking of that. . . . *(Puts sack over, one he's been lying on.* PAL *crosses with two sacks, one at a time.)*

CLITTERHOUSE
Let's have a look at you now. (BADGER *turns and leans back on rail*) You're coming round now.

BADGER
The old heart, ain't it, Guv'nor? (PAL *comes to rail, takes sack which is lying there.)*

CLITTERHOUSE
I'm afraid it is. . . . You've strained it a bit, Badger.

BADGER
I been told that, Guv'nor. But I'm better now. . . .

OAKIE
(Appearing)
Silver foxes now, Guv'nor! (CLITTERHOUSE *takes sack.* OAKIE *goes.* BADGER *takes sack from him.)*

CLITTERHOUSE
(To BADGER)
Take it easy. . . .

BADGER

I can do my bit now. (OAKIE *disappears.* CLITTERHOUSE *brings sacks to rail.* BADGER *tries to help to lift them. Nearly faints again, hangs on to rail.*)

CLITTERHOUSE

I told you to take it easy. (*Puts sack over.*)

PAL

(*At rail*)

We can manage without you, mate. You sit down! . . . Guv'-nor, shall I tell Bert to send up a chair?

BADGER

This ain't the bleeding Ritz! (*Holding on to rail.*)

PAL

Hark at him, Guv'nor. . . .

CLITTERHOUSE

He's got a voice like a lion.

PAL

He's got a heart like one—only it's a bit shaky.

BADGER

My heart's all right! (*Still holding rail.* PAL *takes sacks, one at a time.*)

OAKIE

(*At trap-door with two sacks*)

Here y' are. . . . They're coming quicker now, Guv'nor. . . . Not so far to carry 'em!

134

BADGER

I'll get those. (OAKIE *goes.* CLITTERHOUSE *takes sacks.*)

CLITTERHOUSE

No, no, no! Badger. (CLITTERHOUSE, *at both sacks, does not pick them up.*)

BADGER

Right then! Take it easy!

CLITTERHOUSE

Don't rush it, then! (*Leaves sack to him.* CLITTERHOUSE *climbs railings, goes to back of roof, glances down, then becomes tense.* BADGER *puts one over to* PAL, *who takes it.* BADGER *crosses for other sack.*)

PAL
(*To* BERT *below, listening*)

Eh? What's that? 'Streuth! (*Turning to* CLITTERHOUSE) Guv'nor, my brother Bert says that rozzer's below!

CLITTERHOUSE

I know. . . . I can see him. (PAL *goes on rostrum. Stands beside* CLITTERHOUSE.)

BADGER
(*At rail with sack. Loudly*)

What's that? . . . Copper?

CLITTERHOUSE

Shut up! (BADGER *drops sack, climbs the rails and follows. They stand watching.* BADGER *stands below rostrum. Pause.*)

135

PAL

Think he's rumbled us?

CLITTERHOUSE

I don't know. He's only been there a few moments. (*Pause.*)

PAL

Gaw! How I'd like to drop a brick on him!

BADGER

Why don't he go? (*Pause.* OAKIE *brings one sack. Puts it on ledge. Starts to climb out and makes noise.* CLITTERHOUSE *says "Sh!"*)

OAKIE
(*At trap-door*)

What's up?

PAL

Rozzer! (OAKIE *joins them on rostrum. Pause.*)

OAKIE

Look! Tug's telling him that tale about going to Aldgate.

PAL

Yes . . . but you can't tell if he's taking it! (*Pause.*)

BADGER

The copper keeps looking in through the door. (*Pause.*)

CLITTERHOUSE

I think I'd better go down. (*He goes toward trap.*)

136

OAKIE

Wait a minute, Guv'nor. See how it blows first.

PAL

Hold on, Guv'nor.... I think he's smacked a rumble! (CLIT-
TERHOUSE *goes back on rostrum. A pause.*)

BADGER

I don't like the look o' this! (*Pause.*)

OAKIE

What's he doin' now? (*Pause.*)

BADGER

He's got his notebook out.... It's a rumble.... (*Steps back*)
I'm off! (*Darts across the roof to rail.*)

CLITTERHOUSE

Stop him! (BADGER *is half over rail when* OAKIE *catches him.*
PAL *climbs rail and takes his arm.* PAL *and* BADGER *are now at
right of rail.*)

BADGER

(*Struggling*)

He's on to us. (*Collapsing*) It's a rumble.... I'll get ten
years for this.... (PAL *claps his hand over his mouth.* BADGER
almost faints again.)

OAKIE

Shut up!

CLITTERHOUSE

(*Coming to* OAKIE)

Badger, keep your head. Let me have him, Oakie.... You

watch the street.... (OAKIE *goes to rostrum*. CLITTERHOUSE *holds* BADGER *up*) It's quite all right, Badger. Don't be alarmed, old chap....

BADGER

They got us, Guv'nor.... (*Hanging on to* CLITTERHOUSE'S *coat*.)

PAL

Not yet, they haven't!

CLITTERHOUSE

Listen, Badger! If we do have to bolt, we'll go through the warehouse.... I'll look after you!

BADGER

He had his notebook out, Guv'nor....

OAKIE

Hold hard! ... The copper's going.... Yes, he's moving off! (BADGER *clings to rail*.)

PAL

Honest? (*Climbs over. A pause*.)

OAKIE

Yes. He's gone. (PAL *goes to rostrum*) Gor' Lumme, Tug's fetching out another box.... (BADGER *climbs over rail*.)

CLITTERHOUSE

(*Turning to him*)

There you are, Badger! (CLITTERHOUSE *and* OAKIE *step off rostrum*. BADGER *crosses and looks over rail*.)

138

OAKIE

(*Loudly. Blowing. Steps off rostrum*)
Blimey! That very nigh gave *me* heart disease!

CLITTERHOUSE

(*At rail, to* OAKIE)
You'd better get back to Nobbler, or he'll be wondering
what's happened. (OAKIE *goes over rail and exits.*)

BADGER

(*Looking over rail in old place*)
Copper's gone round the corner now....

CLITTERHOUSE

We expected that policeman, Badger. There was nothing
to get excited about.

PAL

Excited! He was too scared to faint!

BADGER

I've made a fool of myself again.... (*Stumbling to railing*)
I'll make up for it.

CLITTERHOUSE

Stay where you are, Badger.... Take a rest. (BADGER *goes
over rail and crosses to sack on ledge. Pause. Then to cistern
for water.*)

PAL

(*Coming to him. Proudly*)
I never lost me voice that time!

CLITTERHOUSE

I've hooked it up for you! Pal, ask brother Bert what happened. . . .

PAL

(*Taking sack, by rail*)

I will! (*Calls down*) Bert!

OAKIE

Nobbler says another ten minutes, and we'll have cleared the lot!

CLITTERHOUSE

Everything?

OAKIE

All the bleeding lot!

CLITTERHOUSE

Good work! (OAKIE *lifts out two or three more sacks.*)

PAL

(*At little door*)

What's that, Bert? . . . Straight, he did? . . . 'Streuth! (*Comes to left of* CLITTERHOUSE) Guv'nor, that wasn't a notebook the rozzer fetched out!

CLITTERHOUSE

No?

BADGER

It looked like one!

140

PAL

It was a street guide. He was telling Tug the nearest way to Aldgate. (*All laugh and set to work again.* OAKIE *throws out sacks.* BADGER *carries sack to rail.* CLITTERHOUSE *hands sack to* PAL *as*

Curtain falls

ACT TWO

Scene III

SCENE: DAISY'S *flat. The same as Act II, Scene I, at 8:45, the following evening.*

The cocktail cabinet is open. Door is open. Newspapers are strewn on the settee and table, with two or three on the floor.

DAISY *discovered curled up on settee, reading magazine, eating chocolates from box. Doorbell rings. She hides chocolate box under papers and cushion. Rises, goes to door and exits.*

OAKIE

(*Off stage*)

Hello, Daise! Anybody home? (DAISY *enters from the hall, having just admitted* OAKIE, *who follows, closing door.*)

DAISY

This is a fine time for anybody to turn up.

OAKIE

(*In doorway*)

The pay-off isn't till nine o'clock.

DAISY

(*Settles in settee again. Reads magazine*)

I haven't had a word from anybody all day.

OAKIE

You look all right on it, anyhow.

142

DAISY
(Finger on line, reading)
You might have been pinched for all I knew... (OAKIE
pushes his hat to back of his head. Turns) ... and take your
hat off!

OAKIE
All right.... All right, Daise!

DAISY
And don't call me "Daise" either.

OAKIE
(Removes hat)
Here, what's the matter, old girl? *(Puts hat on table.)*

DAISY
I've been up all night.

OAKIE
Why, didn't he ring?

DAISY
Nobody rang.... You all go off on the biggest job you've
ever done and I don't know what happens to you!

OAKIE
(Wagging his head)
It was a big 'un, wasn't it?

DAISY
I've been worried sick.

143

OAKIE

(*Picks up paper from cabinet*)

Seen our notices?

DAISY

I've read the print off the papers.

OAKIE

"Sensational City Robbery. Two Hundred Thousand Pounds in Furs Missing!" Blimey, Daisy, they're worth double since we pinched 'em.

DAISY

(*Angrily*)

Well, how did it go off?

OAKIE

Oh! Like shelling peas! ... (*Throws paper on to desk, notices screwdriver. Pause. Looks at* DAISY) Why, didn't anybody drop in to tell you?

DAISY

(*Reading paper*)

Not a blasted soul.... I'd ha' been glad to see Badger, even.

OAKIE

(*Picks it up*)

Then what's Benny Kellerman's screwdriver doing here? (*Holds out something he has picked off the floor near desk chair.*)

DAISY

I suppose he dropped it. (*She breaks off. Looks up.*)

144

OAKIE

Oh, has he been in then?

DAISY

(*Caught out*)

Yes . . . about an hour ago.

OAKIE

What did he come for?

DAISY

(*Points to magazine on settee*)

He brought me these. . . . (*Drags a box of chocolates from under newspapers on the settee, kneels on settee*) Have one? (*Hands box to him.*)

OAKIE

No, thanks. . . . Why didn't he stop?

DAISY

He's gone to get the money. He just looked in. . . . This was a kind of present.

OAKIE

Oh. . . . (*Blunt.*) Well, you don't want to take things off him, with the guv'nor . . . standing all this for you . . . and don't have Benny up here when you're on your own, neither. It don't do, see. (*Goes to fireplace.*)

DAISY

(*Not looking at him*)

It don't, do it, Oakie? . . . (*Puts box on cabinet.*)

145

OAKIE

No. . . .

DAISY

But I don't like Benny now. . . . (*Arranges her hair back of her head*.)

OAKIE

That's all right then. . . . But he don't like the guv'nor—and he's a vicious devil when he's got a down on a man. (*At fireplace*.)

DAISY

(*Flaring*)

I tell you, I don't like him. But the guv'nor don't intend anything. . . . He uses this place like it was a bloody office!

OAKIE

Well, we got to meet somewhere.

DAISY

(*Gesturing to telephone*)

And he rings up to say he'll be late home, as well!

OAKIE

Well, he's a crook on business lines!

DAISY

Until he's ready for another job, he won't come near here!

OAKIE

Don't worry. I'll look in and see you now and again.

DAISY

What a thrill that'll be! (*Doorbell rings*.)

146

OAKIE

What's that? (OAKIE *turns sharply, jumps nervously*) I've got the jumps after last night. (*Going to door*) Here, Daise! see who it is, and talk aloud.

DAISY

Okay. (*She exits.* OAKIE *stands in kitchen door and listens. Loudly. Offstage*) Hello, Pal!

PAL
(*Loudly. Offstage*)

Hello, Daise! What are you shouting for? Anybody at 'ome? (OAKIE *closes door and returns to fire.*)

DAISY
(*Loudly. Offstage*)

Oakie.

PAL

Come on in, Badger.... (*Enter* PAL *and* BADGER) What, me old Oakie! How are you, Cock! Ah! Ha! The cabinet ain't shut tonight, I see. (PAL *crosses right of cabinet and sits upon end of settee.*)

BADGER
(*Following to behind cabinet*)

Hello, Oakie. (*Cap off and on table.* DAISY *follows and closes door.*)

OAKIE

Watcher, Badger! ... You got away all right, Pal.

PAL
(*Picks up paper from settee*)

'Course we did.... Daise, I'd like a "White Lady."

DAISY

Oh! You'll like a *Martini!*

PAL

Help yourself to a cigar, Badger.

BADGER

(*Above cabinet, takes cigar. Smells it, puts it in pocket*)
Haven't you got any beer, Daise? (DAISY *goes to cabinet.*)

OAKIE
(*Being very refined*)
Oh, no, mate. There ain't any beer *here,* mate.

PAL
(*Imitating* OAKIE)
No! It don't smell nice, Badger. (*Changing to his usual way of speaking*) Give him the same as me, Daise.

BADGER

Oh, well. Make it whisky then, if you got any.

DAISY

What's for you, Oakie? (DAISY *pours drinks.*)

OAKIE
(*Goes up a step*)
I'll wait for the guv'nor.

PAL
(*Picks up paper from floor*)
Blimey, you got some papers here! Ha! Ha! They ain't on to us, though—I've been reading 'em. . . .

BADGER

One paper says the coppers is er—baffled. (*Points with index finger, trying to find the word.*)

PAL

(*Reaching for paper on pouffe*)
Thank Gawd for that! (DAISY *puts* BADGER's *drink on cabinet.*)

DAISY

(*She hands* PAL *his. Crosses and sits in the armchair*)
Here you are, Pal.

PAL

Ta!

BADGER

(*Taking drink from cabinet and raising glass*)
Well, here's looking for more luck!

PAL

Rot him! (*Raises hat as usual. Both drink.*)

OAKIE

How you feeling now, Badger?

BADGER

Oh! I'm all right. . . . I fainted on the job last night, Daise.

DAISY

Did you?

PAL

Yes, it was through chucking them sacks about. . . . The guv'nor fetched him round, though.

BADGER

Good sort, ain't he?

OAKIE

Good sort! I'll say so. The way he had everything tapped was a caution.... Even to that copper!

PAL

I'll bet that copper's fed up now.

BADGER

If he'd ha' known, eh?

PAL

One toot on his whistle—and we'd have been askin' for a kind-hearted judge! ... Rot him—whoever he might have been. (*Raises hat again.*)

DAISY

Was that the copper you expected?

OAKIE

It was.

DAISY

(*Angrily*)

Well, what happened?

OAKIE

Yes, and what d'you think? ... He took out his notebook and told Tug the nearest way to Aldgate. (*All laugh.* DAISY *makes a sudden gesture, listening.*)

150

DAISY

Hello!

PAL

Somebody with a key. (*All become tense.* PAL *rises,* BADGER *puts glass on cabinet.*)

DAISY

It's all right—it's him! (*Exit* DAISY. *Leaves door open, calling off stage*) Hello, dear! (*Others relax on hearing* CLITTERHOUSE'S *voice.*)

CLITTERHOUSE
(*Off stage*)

Hello, Daisy. (*Entering with bag, goes to desk*) Good evening, gentlemen.... I hope I see you all well. (*Puts bag on end of desk.*)

PAL

In the pink, Guv'nor! (DAISY *closes door, following* CLITTERHOUSE.)

BADGER

I'm grand!

OAKIE

Wot cheer, China! Everybody got away all right....

DAISY

You might have rung me up.

CLITTERHOUSE
(*Pats her on shoulder*)

At times like these, even the telephone is dangerous. Have you seen the papers? (*Picks up paper from settee.*)

151

OAKIE

We've seen all of them.

BADGER

(*Anxiously*)

You ain't seen anything in them about us?

CLITTERHOUSE

They've found out how it was done.

OTHERS

(*Startled*)

What!!

CLITTERHOUSE

But the great thing is that they don't know who did it.

DAISY

Will you have something?

CLITTERHOUSE

No. I'll wait a little while. ... (*Puts paper down*) How are you, Badger?

BADGER

There's nothing wrong with me now, Guv'nor.

CLITTERHOUSE

D'you mind if I have a look at you?

PAL

Here, Guv'nor! (*Rising eagerly*) Are you going to have his blood?

CLITTERHOUSE

No. Sit down here, Badger, and take your coat off. (*Pulling desk chair out, facing* BADGER. DAISY *goes behind* BADGER *and takes coat. Puts coat on table, then drops to behind cabinet.*)

BADGER

(*Sits in chair*)

What are you going to do?

CLITTERHOUSE

(*Producing stethoscope from hip pocket*)

I'm going to pretend that I'm a real doctor, and give you a little free advice.

PAL

He won't hurt you, mate!

BADGER

(*Leaning forward. To* PAL)

I'm all right now!

CLITTERHOUSE

(*Taking his arm and seating him in chair*)

Of course you're all right, Badger.... But we can't have you fainting all over the place. Undo that, will you? (PAL *sits on arm of settee, grinning.*)

BADGER

(*Opening shirt*)

I didn't mean it, last night, Guv'nor.

153

CLITTERHOUSE

(*Puts on stethoscope*)

Of course you didn't.... Don't worry over it.... Keep quiet now. (*A silence. Starts to sound him.* BADGER *very frightened.*)

PAL

Go on, Guv'nor. Have a go at his throat.

DAISY

(*Above cabinet*)

Shut up!

CLITTERHOUSE

(*Looking up*)

Badger, it's all right, you know.... There's no need to be nervous. (*Sounds him again.*)

BADGER

(*Nervously*)

I ain't scared, Guv'nor. (*Pause.*)

CLITTERHOUSE

(*Straightens up. Stethoscope out of one ear*)

Give him a whisky, Daisy. You've had one, haven't you, Badger?

DAISY

Take it straight? (BADGER *nods. All are watching.* DAISY *pours drink.*)

PAL

Go on, Guv! Go down his throat—I'd like to watch that! (DAISY *glares at him from cabinet. Pause.*)

154

CLITTERHOUSE
(Stethoscope round neck. Takes whisky from DAISY *and hands
it to* BADGER)
Here you are, Badger. *(Studies him.)*

BADGER
Best respects, Guv'nor! (BADGER *drinks.)*

OAKIE
He's strong enough to push a bus over, isn't he?

PAL
'Course! Two buses!

CLITTERHOUSE
(Turns and puts stethoscope on desk)
Yes, but he's been overdoing things a bit, that's all. D'you
hear what I say, Badger?

BADGER
Yes, Guv'nor....

CLITTERHOUSE
You must take it easy.... No excitement.

BADGER
I know what you mean.

CLITTERHOUSE
(Producing notes from bag)
Look here, I'll give you your cut now.... I brought it in
case we had a chance to talk before Kellerman arrived. (BADGER
rises) Here you are—five hundred. (PAL *looks at* OAKIE *in
approval.)*

BADGER

My cut's only three!

CLITTERHOUSE

I know. But that's a bit extra because we did well.... And I've got something else for you too. (*Brings a small tube from his pocket*) Just take one of these when you feel a little groggy.

BADGER

(*Dubiously, as he puts notes in his trousers pocket*) What are they?

CLITTERHOUSE

Tablets.... (BADGER *takes tube*) You'd do well to keep away from that as much as possible.... (*Nodding to whisky.* BADGER *goes to hand glass to* DAISY. *But finishes drink. Hands glass empty. She puts it on cabinet*) Just take one at a time!

BADGER

(*Adjusting shirt*)

Yes, Guv'nor.

CLITTERHOUSE

Now have you got anywhere you can go ... in the country?

BADGER

I've got a sister married a bus driver, Margate way.

CLITTERHOUSE

Why not pay her a visit—for as long as you can?

BADGER

Well, I might.... It's my heart, ain't it, Guv'nor?

CLITTERHOUSE

You've got a grand heart, Badger, but only it's not working quite as well as it should.

BADGER

I know. Well, I s'pose I might as well be moving along. Good-bye, Guv'nor. (CLITTERHOUSE *holds out his hand*.)

CLITTERHOUSE

Good-bye, Badger.

BADGER

Thanks for the cut . . . and thanks for the job. . . . (DAISY *brings coat and helps him on*) So long, Daise. . . .

DAISY

(*Helping him with coat*)

Good-bye, Badger.

BADGER

Well, don't get picked up, mates! (*Crosses to door. Picks up cap.*)

PAL

(*Round cabinet. To* BADGER)

We'll be seeing you, Badger! (*Pats him on back*)

OAKIE

Best o' luck, China.

BADGER

Well, so long, Guv'nor. . . .

CLITTERHOUSE

(*Putting stethoscope in bag. Then watches him off*)
Good-bye, and remember what I told you!

BADGER

Yes! I'll remember.

CLITTERHOUSE

No more excitement.

BADGER

No.... (*Forcing smile*) It ain't good for me, is it? (*Opens door*) Well, good luck, everybody! (BADGER *exits.*)

OAKIE

What's he got, Guv'nor?

CLITTERHOUSE

(*Coming to front of cabinet*)
D'you really want to know? (DAISY *stays near door*)

DAISY

Tell us....

CLITTERHOUSE

Three months, if I'm any judge.

OAKIE

Poor old Badger....

DAISY

(*Keenly, to* CLITTERHOUSE)
You're a real doctor, ain't you?

158

CLITTERHOUSE

(*Turns to her*)

What makes you think that? (*Looks at watch*) Where is Tug? And isn't Nobbler coming? (*Crosses to fire.*)

OAKIE

They'll be here in a minute.... What's the time?

DAISY

Nearly nine.

PAL

What's happened to them? (*They glance at one another.*)

DAISY

Tug always gets here first—when there's a cut.

PAL

He wouldn't have been picked up, would he?

OAKIE

No!

CLITTERHOUSE

There's no reason to think that.... We didn't slip up anywhere. (*Bell rings.* PAL *goes quickly to door and opens it.* OAKIE *rises and quickly crosses in front of* CLITTERHOUSE) Would that be Tug? (DAISY *quickly exits into hall.*)

OAKIE

It ought to be Benny.... The other would come in the back way!

DAISY
(*Off stage*)

Oh, here you are!

KELLERMAN
(*Off stage*)

Hello, Daise!

CLITTERHOUSE

It's Kellerman. (PAL *and* OAKIE *relax.*)

OAKIE

Thank God! (*Pats* PAL *on back.*)

PAL
(*Coming back*)

What's happened to them others?

CLITTERHOUSE

Oh, they'll be coming soon!

OAKIE

You bet they will—with the cuts they got coming! (KELLER-
MAN *enters with small suitcase and paper. His manner appears ominous.*)

KELLERMAN
(*Puts case on cabinet*)

Well, you **won't** see Tug and Nobbler here tonight!

CLITTERHOUSE

Why not?

160

PAL

What's up?

OAKIE

What's happened? (DAISY *re-enters.*)

KELLERMAN
(*To* CLITTERHOUSE)
I've given them their cuts, and got them away....

CLITTERHOUSE

What do you mean?

KELLERMAN

I got scared when Tug told me about that copper. He must have had a damn good look at him!

CLITTERHOUSE

Oh....

KELLERMAN

He's given a description. It's in all the papers now!...Take a look at that! (*Hands newspaper to* CLITTERHOUSE.)

CLITTERHOUSE
(*Reading*)
"Sensational City robbery. Description of wanted man...." (*Looking up*) This might be anybody....

OAKIE

Let's have a look, Guv'nor.... (CLITTERHOUSE *passes paper across.* DAISY *drops down, pushes* PAL *aside and stands between them. All behind settee.* DAISY *and* PAL *read it with him.*)

KELLERMAN

Well, I reckoned it was best to play safe, so I got them away quick. The Tecs is checking up on everybody—good crooks and bad.... Asking questions, see?

OAKIE
(*Tapping paper*)

Tug wouldn't recognize himself! And he's shaved his moustache off now.

CLITTERHOUSE
(*Looking at own paper*)

You think that policeman would know him again?

KELLERMAN

Know him? ... That cop's got a grudge! I've had a day of it, I can tell you. (*Stops and turns*) Three times they've been into my place, to see who they can pick up!

PAL

What have you done with the stuff?

KELLERMAN

It was on its way out of the country before morning. (*Looks casually at phone.*)

CLITTERHOUSE

That's rapid!

KELLERMAN

You got to be rapid! ... Here, where's Badger?

CLITTERHOUSE

He's been, and gone again.

KELLERMAN

Got him away, too?

CLITTERHOUSE

Yes.

KELLERMAN

That's good. We don't want any of 'em back until this thing blows over. When the cops is picking up anybody, that's the time to be extra careful!

OAKIE

(*Throws paper on settee and crosses to* KELLERMAN)
But, we've all got stone-ginger alibis. Now look here, I was with you and Punch—the whole of last night.

KELLERMAN

That's right.

PAL

Me and my brother Bert was home—and fast asleep. We don't even know what a fur looks like!

CLITTERHOUSE

We left no clues at all, and we never took a glove off, the whole time. (*Sits upon settee, with paper.*)

KELLERMAN

Oh, it's all right—can't be anything else! Well, let's have a drink. Then we'll take a look at this. (*Takes bag from cabinet, goes behind settee.* OAKIE *crosses to desk.*)

DAISY

What'll you have?

KELLERMAN

Whisky straight.

CLITTERHOUSE

Dry Martini for me. (*Still looking at paper.*)

PAL

And me!

OAKIE

(*Sits on desk*)

I'll have one too.

DAISY

Then I'll join in! (*She pours drinks.* PAL *takes his from cabinet.*)

CLITTERHOUSE

(*Looking up*)

That should cheer things up a little. You came in with a face like Fate, Mr. Kellerman.

KELLERMAN

I've got a funny feeling about this job. . . .

OAKIE

Well, it's all over now—bar paying!

KELLERMAN

I've never liked it from the start. . . . I've got all the stuff away. . . . I've collected my dough—but still I've got a feeling.

DAISY

(*Passing glass to* KELLERMAN)

Here, chase it off with this!

164

PAL

A feeling o' what?

KELLERMAN

I don't know....

CLITTERHOUSE

It's nervous reaction, that's all. (*Throwing paper down.*)

KELLERMAN

If I knew more about you, I'd feel safer!

CLITTERHOUSE

I wonder if you would.... (DAISY *gives him glass.*)

KELLERMAN

What d'you mean by that?

CLITTERHOUSE

Your very good health! (*Raising glass. Smiling.*)

KELLERMAN

Why *don't* you open up a bit?

DAISY

Oh, don't start all that again, Benny.

KELLERMAN
(*To* CLITTERHOUSE)

Well, I don't like working in the dark.

CLITTERHOUSE

No. You have hinted that.

OAKIE
(*Raising glass*)
Well, here's to the next time, Guv'nor!

DAISY
Cheerio!

CLITTERHOUSE
Crime—and research!

PAL
Rot him! (*Raising hat. They drink.* PAL's, DAISY's *and* CLITTERHOUSE's *glasses on cabinet.* CLITTERHOUSE *does not empty his.* KELLERMAN's *glass on pouffe.*)

CLITTERHOUSE
How have you brought it? (KELLERMAN *puts bag on a settee and opens it.*)

KELLERMAN
I paid Tug and Nobbler a thousand, in packets of five hundred each apiece, and that leaves you twelve thousand quid.

DAISY
You sound like a bank, Benny!

OAKIE
Blimey! If some of the boys had known you was carrying that!

PAL
You wouldn't have got here. . . .

166

CLITTERHOUSE
(*Counting bundles*)
Well, here's yours, Pal.... (*Passes one bundle over settee.*)

PAL
Thanks, Guv'. Fifteen hundred.... It's a gift.

CLITTERHOUSE
And brother Bert's.... Five hundred. (*Throws one bundle across.*)

PAL
Ta! (*He splits bundles and puts notes in different pockets.*)

OAKIE
If the rozzers could see us now!

CLITTERHOUSE
Oh, Daisy.... This is for you! (*Hands her a wad of notes.* KELLERMAN *turns.*)

DAISY
O-oh! ... I didn't expect this!

CLITTERHOUSE
Well, that's a present for being a good girl.

DAISY
Oh, it's ever so nice of you. (*She hugs him and kisses his cheek.*)

CLITTERHOUSE
Daisy! ... You'll embarrass our friends. (KELLERMAN *is watching.*)

167

PAL
(Lighting cigarette)

Don't mind us!

CLITTERHOUSE

Here you are, Oakie. (OAKIE *takes bag from him across cabinet and takes it to table*) Help yourself. Daisy, put the rest in my bag, will you?

DAISY
(Crossing to desk for his bag)

Yes, dear.

OAKIE

You do trust me, don't you?

CLITTERHOUSE

I do. (OAKIE *and* DAISY *become busy over the suitcase.* OAKIE *takes notes for himself and turns away from table, leaving* DAISY *to transfer the rest.*)

KELLERMAN

Well, are you thinking of easing off now?

CLITTERHOUSE

Yes....

PAL

How long for?

CLITTERHOUSE

I don't know ... quite. *(Reaching behind him for glass.)*
168

KELLERMAN
(*To* CLITTERHOUSE)
I thought perhaps you might be.

OAKIE
(*Putting notes away*)
Oh, why?

KELLERMAN
Oh, just an idea I had. (DAISY *puts* CLITTERHOUSE'S *bag on cabinet, then crosses behind to left of settee.*)

CLITTERHOUSE
(*Drinks, puts glass on cabinet*)
Well, I think that's all for the present. I must be getting along. (*Goes toward door. Pauses, then to phone. Sits in chair at desk.* DAISY *comes to warn* CLITTERHOUSE *not to use phone, but* KELLERMAN *catches her wrist as she passes him.* OAKIE, *behind cabinet, sees this.*)

KELLERMAN
Well, the best thing for everyone now is to keep quiet for a bit. (*Releasing her wrist.*)

CLITTERHOUSE
(*Dialing*)
Yes—stay around and act normally.

DAISY
Are you going now?

CLITTERHOUSE
I'm afraid so.

DAISY

Coming up tomorrow?

CLITTERHOUSE

I don't think I can promise you that, Daisy ... but I'll be seeing you.

DAISY

When? (DAISY *turns and looks at* KELLERMAN, *then slowly sits on settee.*)

CLITTERHOUSE
(*Into phone*)

Hello. Yes, it is. Telephone immediately and say I'll be there in twenty minutes. Then I'll come straight back. That's all. Good-bye. (*Replaces phone. Rises*) I'm afraid I'll have to be getting along.

OAKIE

What about the next job, Guv'nor?

CLITTERHOUSE

No, not now, Oakie!

DAISY
(*To* CLITTERHOUSE)

Well, I'll get them all here when you want them next time.

CLITTERHOUSE

Yes! Yes! Of course. (*Takes bag from cabinet*) Well, I'm afraid you'll have to excuse me.

170

PAL
(*Rises*)
Oh! Have another before you go!

CLITTERHOUSE
No, thanks, I really must be getting along. Good-bye, Mr. Kellerman. Cheerio, Pal!

PAL

So long, Guv'!

CLITTERHOUSE
Good-bye, Oakie. (*Shakes hands*) You've backed me up splendidly.

DAISY
(*Rises*)

I'll see you out.

CLITTERHOUSE
(*Opening door*)
Thanks, Daisy.

PAL

Be seein' you, Guv'nor!

CLITTERHOUSE
Yes. (CLITTERHOUSE *exits.* DAISY *follows.*)

OAKIE
(*Calling through door*)
Good luck, China.

CLITTERHOUSE
(Off stage)

Good-bye! (OAKIE *closes door. A little silence.* PAL *sits on chair, chin on hand.*)

KELLERMAN

Bit of a hurry, wasn't he?

OAKIE

Oh, well, he's got his own friends.

KELLERMAN
(Crosses to behind cabinet. Helps himself to a drink)

Tcha! Have one, Oakie?

OAKIE

No. (DAISY *returns. Closes door, leans against it.*)

DAISY

Well, he's gone....

PAL

He hopped it quick....

KELLERMAN

Yes... and d'you know what he's doing? It looks to me like (*Finishes drink, puts glass down on cabinet*) he's dropping you.

DAISY

Dropping ... me?

KELLERMAN

All of you....

172

OAKIE

Not him!

KELLERMAN

You'll see....

PAL

He's all right.... I'll take me oath on that!

KELLERMAN

Would you! Well, I want to know a bit more about him.
(*Goes toward telephone.*)

OAKIE

(*Pause.* OAKIE *and* PAL *look at each other*)
Here, what are you getting at, Benny?

KELLERMAN

You wait and see.... (*Fumbles in his pockets.*)

OAKIE

Hello, lost something? (DAISY *crosses slowly to settee.*)

KELLERMAN

I had a screwdriver. (OAKIE *and* DAISY *turn and look at each
other.*)

OAKIE

(*Producing it*)
Is this it?... You dropped it when you was in here
before.... (PAL *looks up at this.*)

173

KELLERMAN

(*Coolly*)

Oh, did I? ... Thanks, Oakie. (*Takes screwdriver.*)

PAL

(*Rises. To* OAKIE)

Has he been here earlier on?

OAKIE

(*Both glancing at* DAISY)

Yes.... (*To* KELLERMAN) Here, what are you doing? (PAL *continues to look at* DAISY, *who has not looked up at all.*)

KELLERMAN

(*Working at telephone*)

He always telephones someone before he goes.... He isn't the only clever one! (*Pries off the paper disc on the dialing plate, then unscrews plate itself.*)

PAL

What are you after, Benny? (*Watches him work on phone.*)

OAKIE

Here, Daisy ... have you two rigged up something against the Guv'nor?

DAISY

(*Rather feebly*)

I want to know who he is, the same as Benny.

OAKIE

I don't like the look of this, Pal.

174

PAL

Nor me ... neither.

KELLERMAN

I know what I'm doing. (*Removes the dialing plate and lifts a small, white ring from beneath*) I worked in a watchmaker's years ago, and I haven't forgotten how to handle the small stuff. ...

PAL

Daise, what's he done to the telephone?

OAKIE
(*To* DAISY)

Here, what's the lay?

DAISY

He put that underneath when he came before.

OAKIE

What is it?

DAISY

I dunno!

KELLERMAN

I'll tell you.... (PAL *crosses to his right.* OAKIE *crosses to his left.* KELLERMAN *at the dialing plate*) I fitted a little scriber underneath this plate.... (*Puts plate on desk.*)

PAL

What for?

KELLERMAN

It worked against this ring.... When the dial spun, the scriber left a mark, then clicked back a notch.... Got the idea? (*To* OAKIE.)

OAKIE

No.... And I don't like the sound of it!

KELLERMAN

(*Turns on him*)

That worries me! ... I've got myself to look after.

DAISY

(*Still sitting*)

What does the thing do, anyway?

KELLERMAN

(*Puts watchmaker's glass in eye and examines ring*)

Well! The scriber goes round with the dial and makes a mark each time.... It's made seven marks altogether—and I can tell by the length of them what number he called.

PAL

Blimey! (KELLERMAN *produces a second dialing plate, returns to the telephone and begins to screw it home.*)

OAKIE

Aw! What good will that do you? (PAL, *above desk, watches* KELLERMAN.)

DAISY

You'll only start a packet of trouble, Benny!

176

KELLERMAN

I told him I didn't like working in the dark.... Now we'll have a bit of light.... (*Puts watchmaker's glass in eye. Compares the adjusted dialing plate with the ring and begins slowly to dial a number.* OAKIE *crosses stealthily, looks over his shoulder, watches him dial.*)

OAKIE

Here, Benny, are you ringing that number?

KELLERMAN

I am....

DAISY
(*Rises*)

I wish you wouldn't, Benny!

PAL

It looks too tricky to me.

OAKIE

Why don't you lay off it? (*Crosses to cabinet. Faces* DAISY) It can't do any good!

KELLERMAN
(*With receiver at ear*)

You leave this to me.... (*All wait.* KELLERMAN *snaps his fingers, then nods. They all react to "Got it!" and again to, "Doctor whose residence?"*) Got it! (OAKIE *turns quickly. Transfers receiver to right hand, puts white ring in waistcoat pocket*) Hello, who's that? ... Who is it? ... Doctor whose residence? (PAL *drops to above desk.* OAKIE *takes a step toward* KELLERMAN) Oh, sorry.... Wrong number! (*Slowly replaces the receiver.*)

DAISY

(*After receiver is replaced*)

D'you know who he is?

KELLERMAN

Yes. . . . (*Turns*) Yes, I do. . . . (*His manner is grim as he looks at them*) Now I'll have a bit o' fun! (DAISY *sits down slowly.*)

Curtain

ACT THREE

ACT THREE

Scene I

Scene: DR. CLITTERHOUSE's *consulting room, just after dark, next evening.*

SIR WILLIAM GRANT, K.C., *discovered lying on couch.*

CLITTERHOUSE *bends over him with stethoscope. Then he moves to desk for ophthalmoscope.*

CLITTERHOUSE

Thank you, Sir William. Sit up! Won't you! (SIR WILLIAM *sits up.* CLITTERHOUSE *switches lamp out.*)

CLITTERHOUSE

Quite still, please.... (*Examines right eye*) One moment longer. (*Examines left eye*) Thank you, Sir William. (CLITTERHOUSE *crosses to left, switches lights on and returns to foot of couch. Switches ophthalmoscope off.* SIR WILLIAM *runs his fingertips over his eyes.*)

SIR WILLIAM

Well, what's the verdict? (CLITTERHOUSE *glances at him, amused*) Anything serious?

CLITTERHOUSE

You have been spending a little too much time at the bar, my learned friend.

SIR WILLIAM

Well, can I put on my coat now?

CLITTERHOUSE

Yes, do.

SIR WILLIAM

Thanks! (SIR WILLIAM *puts coat on.* CLITTERHOUSE *puts oph-thalmoscope on couch and washes hands at cabinet.*)

CLITTERHOUSE

Tell me, have you been working very hard?

SIR WILLIAM

Yes, on the Maynard case.... Thank heavens, it's over.

CLITTERHOUSE

And over very brilliantly for you!... But we expect that.... Was he innocent? (*Closes cupboard. Picks up ophthalmoscope.*)

SIR WILLIAM

Yes! We were discussing my headaches!

CLITTERHOUSE

I beg your pardon. Well, don't be alarmed, it's a touch of—

SIR WILLIAM

Alcoholic cirrhosis?

CLITTERHOUSE

Not quite that—just liver ... you've let yourself become over-tired.... You've been obliged to use stimulants.... And now, I'm afraid you are paying for it with headaches.

SIR WILLIAM

My head has been pretty bad, Clitterhouse.

182

CLITTERHOUSE

I know.... Look here.... There is nothing whatever to worry about. I want to make that quite clear.

SIR WILLIAM

Thank you.

CLITTERHOUSE

Now, can you forget legal matters for two or three days?

SIR WILLIAM

Of course, if you advise it.

CLITTERHOUSE

Good. I should like you to take a walk this evening—once round the outer circle in the park....

SIR WILLIAM

I will.

CLITTERHOUSE

And tomorrow morning, do nine holes ... lunch at clubhouse ... and finish the round in the afternoon.

SIR WILLIAM

Um! That will be taking things very easily.

CLITTERHOUSE

Yes, very gentle exercise. (*Puts ophthalmoscope on desk*) But do a full eighteen the day after—and then you should be ready for anything.

SIR WILLIAM

It sounds simple enough.

CLITTERHOUSE

(*Sitting at desk chair*)

That's because I put it to patients as you put it to a jury—very clearly. . . . They are so dull witted.

SIR WILLIAM

That's good!

CLITTERHOUSE

(*Writing prescription*)

Actually, my advice is merely common-sense, only you fellows will pay fees to be told.

SIR WILLIAM

Fortunately for you, eh?

CLITTERHOUSE

Ah-ha! . . . I'll give you a little prescription to help matters on.

SIR WILLIAM

Oh! How about diet?

CLITTERHOUSE

Light and plain . . . for the next week. . . .

SIR WILLIAM

All right.

CLITTERHOUSE

Just take one before you go to bed tonight. (SIR WILLIAM *rises.* CLITTERHOUSE *blots prescription and tears it out*) Leave that at the chemists' to be made up while you take your walk. (CLITTERHOUSE *folds prescription. Hands it over.*)

184

SIR WILLIAM
(*Reading prescription*)
I'll do just as you've told me.

CLITTERHOUSE
(*Rises. Rounds desk*)
If you went out of commission—some of these criminal cases would not be half so interesting....I followed the Maynard affair.

SIR WILLIAM
A little ticklish, that, but I knew we should get him off.

CLITTERHOUSE
You did? I thought conviction was absolutely certain!

SIR WILLIAM
Well, I diagnose from facts just as you diagnose from symptoms.

CLITTERHOUSE
I'm afraid I'd never considered it like that....

SIR WILLIAM
(*Putting prescription away*)
Once I know all the facts, it's reasonably possible to tell what the outcome of a case will be.

CLITTERHOUSE
Even in criminal cases?

SIR WILLIAM
Yes....You can't beat facts. (CLITTERHOUSE *crosses, presses desk-button*) Even if you can overcome an alcoholic liver!

185

CLITTERHOUSE

That's relatively easy.... Nervous strain was at the bottom of your indisposition. (ANN *enters. Stands at door.*)

SIR WILLIAM

I have been going at it lately.

CLITTERHOUSE

Well, good-bye, Sir William. (*Shakes hands.*)

SIR WILLIAM

Good-bye!

CLITTERHOUSE

Remember what I've told you!

SIR WILLIAM
(*Going to door*)

Any excuse for golf is a good one....

CLITTERHOUSE

What's your handicap?

SIR WILLIAM
(*Turns in door*)

Twelve.... What's yours?

CLITTERHOUSE

Oh, I still play for the exercise.... Good-bye.

SIR WILLIAM

Good-bye. (SIR WILLIAM *exits with* ANN. CLITTERHOUSE *crosses above coffee table, lights pipe by fireside.* ANN *re-enters, with newspapers.*)

ANN

An evening paper, Doctor.

CLITTERHOUSE

Oh! Thank you. Have I any more appointments for this evening?

ANN

No, Doctor.

CLITTERHOUSE
(*Scanning paper*)
No. . . . I haven't. . . . Have I. . . . Ah! (*Reads on an inside page, frowning a little before he smiles*) That's good. . . . Isn't it, Nurse?

ANN

Isn't what, doctor?

CLITTERHOUSE
(*Turns*)
Oh, nothing! Is there anything else? (*Folds paper back at page he has been reading.*)

ANN

You asked me to remind you about the heroin for Mrs. Crawford. A fresh supply came in this morning and I put it away.

CLITTERHOUSE

Oh, yes. Let me have it now, will you? (*Goes above coffee table, paper under arm.* ANN *goes to cupboard and returns with*

187

small package, which CLITTERHOUSE *opens*) Has Nurse Harvey telephoned?

ANN

Yes. Her patient was out for a little while this afternoon.

CLITTERHOUSE

And she thought we were going to lose the old buffer. He'll be playing *football* before he's finished. (*Takes one phial from package and reads*) Twelve tablets ... one twelfth grain. I'll keep this out. Lock the rest away, will you? (*Gives her his keys.* ANN *crosses to cupboard*) She has one tablet, if she needs any more tonight, give them one out of this.

ANN

Are you going out then, Doctor? (*Locking cupboard above wash cabinet.*)

CLITTERHOUSE

(*Crossing to front of desk. Puts phial on desk*)
I was forgetting ... I've got an evening to myself, haven't I? Well, I've some writing to do. (*Paper on desk. Takes manuscript book from drawer.*)

ANN

(*Hands keys across desk*)
Your notes, Doctor?

CLITTERHOUSE

Yes.... (*Unlocking his manuscript book*) I've a lot to digest here— (*Riffles the pages.*)

ANN

It's almost full....

188

CLITTERHOUSE

Yes ... I've discovered some things that are very interesting.

ANN

I've always been so afraid that you'd be caught. ...

CLITTERHOUSE

I've been very careful. ...

ANN

But I've always known when you were doing something.

CLITTERHOUSE

Have you? How?

ANN

I could ... I could tell.

CLITTERHOUSE

Oh? ... (*Curiously*) Have you noticed anything lately?

ANN

You've been very anxious to see the papers.

CLITTERHOUSE

Yes! I have, haven't I? (*Picks up paper*) There's something in this one. Got it? (*Hands paper.*)

ANN

(*Reading*)

"Receipt of seven thousand pounds ... anonymous ... Police orphanage?"

CLITTERHOUSE

Yes, I gave another lot to the Prisoners' Aid Society, but I thought that was rather selfish of me, though.

ANN

In case you might ever need their assistance?

CLITTERHOUSE

That was the idea....

ANN

Doctor! Don't you think you've done enough now? Couldn't you give it up? I should feel so much happier.

CLITTERHOUSE

Why?...It doesn't affect you, Nurse!

ANN

Yes! But it does.

CLITTERHOUSE

How?

ANN

Sometimes you appear so tired....

CLITTERHOUSE

Well—late nights.

ANN

So fagged out in the mornings....

CLITTERHOUSE

Oh! Well I'll get an early night tonight, anyway. (*Pause.*

190

Looks at ANN) Well, I think that's all. Thank you, Nurse. Good night! (*Reaches for phone. Dials.*)

ANN

Good night, Doctor. (ANN *goes to door.*)

CLITTERHOUSE
(*Dialing*)

You can go out, you know, if you want to.

ANN

Oh! I should like to run over to see Nurse Harvey presently.

CLITTERHOUSE

Then do.... (*A bell rings in the hall.*)

ANN

Thank you, Doctor. (ANN *exits.*)

CLITTERHOUSE

Hello.... Oh, is Inspector Charles available.... Doctor Clitterhouse speaking. Thank you. (ANN *enters.*)

ANN

Oh, Doctor, can you see someone?

CLITTERHOUSE

Who?

ANN

A Mr. Benjamin.

CLITTERHOUSE

A patient?

ANN

You've never attended him.... But he says it's rather urgent.

CLITTERHOUSE

Hello, Charley! How are you, old man? (*He signs "Bring him in." She exits*) As a matter of fact, I'm not—so I thought I'd ring you up and apologize for not being home the other evening.... Well, we must have a night out, Charley— Too much work is not good for any policeman.... I've just seen your name in the paper, in connection with that fur robbery. It reminded me to ring you up.... Yes, it sounded a big one. Have you got anybody yet? Oh! Well, when you have an... (ANN *enters followed by* KELLERMAN.)

ANN

Mr. Benjamin. (KELLERMAN *crosses to left of chair.*)

CLITTERHOUSE

...evening free, let me know. And you can detail six of your biggest policemen to bring me home.... So long, old boy.... Good-bye! (CLITTERHOUSE *replaces receiver. Looks up. Pauses.* KELLERMAN *chuckles*) Thank you, Nurse. (ANN *goes and* KEL-LERMAN *doesn't speak until she has closed the door.*)

KELLERMAN

Bit of a surprise for you, isn't it?

CLITTERHOUSE
(*Rises*)

Perhaps you would be good enough to explain how you come to be here?

KELLERMAN

Just an idea of my own.... You're not the only smart one.
... So you're a proper doctor, are you?

CLITTERHOUSE

Does anyone else know who I am?

KELLERMAN
(Goes to couch. Puts hat on it)
No. I've kept it to myself—so far.

CLITTERHOUSE

And what do you want?

KELLERMAN

I always knew you weren't one of us....

CLITTERHOUSE

Oh, you did, did you?

KELLERMAN

Just a sort of amateur, aren't you?

CLITTERHOUSE
(Evenly)
I dislike that term, Mr. Kellerman.

KELLERMAN

Don't come that with me.... It don't go any more.

CLITTERHOUSE

I asked you what you wanted here....

KELLERMAN

I heard you. . . . Well, when I know what your game is—then I'll know just how safe you are.

CLITTERHOUSE

Or—putting it more clearly—how safe *you* are.

KELLERMAN

Have it that way if you like. . . . You're a doctor. . . . Unless you've done something to get yourself into trouble, you don't have to steal. . . .

CLITTERHOUSE

Oh. . . .

KELLERMAN

What's all this medical stuff you've been putting across? . . . Taking samples o' blood . . . (*Pointing*) using that thing!

CLITTERHOUSE

(*Pointing to ophthalmoscope on desk*)

That?

KELLERMAN

Yes. . . .

CLITTERHOUSE

Ophthalmoscope. (KELLERMAN *is* *calculating*. CLITTERHOUSE *is very watchful as they regard each other*.)

KELLERMAN

Come on, open up! . . . What's the game?

194

CLITTERHOUSE

Well, I've told you, many times.... Crime—and research!

KELLERMAN

What's that mean?

CLITTERHOUSE

Well, since you're here, I don't mind explaining.... (*Lifting book*) You see this book?...It's almost filled with what I might term my medical notes.

KELLERMAN

What are they for?

CLITTERHOUSE

I intend them as the basis of a book which may or may not reveal why crooks are—crooks, and why they continue to be crooks.

KELLERMAN

(*Steps to front of chair*)

Well, that don't make sense to me. (*Turns to desk again*) Here, what's in that book there?

CLITTERHOUSE

Notes on everything I've done....

KELLERMAN

About the big job, for instance?

CLITTERHOUSE

Well, that's included.... (*Puts book on desk in front of him.*)

195

KELLERMAN

Suppose the cops was to get hold of that?

CLITTERHOUSE

That's very unlikely!

KELLERMAN

But they'll read the book when it's written! You don't know the Tecs like I do! They'll ask a million questions. . . . 'Ere. (KELLERMAN *snatches book, then crosses to coffee table*) Let's have a look at that!

CLITTERHOUSE

Be careful what you're doing, Mr. Kellerman!

KELLERMAN

Think I'm like the others, afraid of you? I always knew you was dangerous. (*Opening book*) My oath, it's lucky I'm tumbling to you. What the 'ell is all this?

CLITTERHOUSE

I'm doubtful if you'll understand it. . . .

KELLERMAN

There's something here though . . . (*Reading*) "P. hit officer, during escape, about 8:45 . . . officer reported killed 9:15. P. immediately subjected to laryngeal spasm . . ." can't make out the rest. What is it—Latin?

CLITTERHOUSE

(*Rises and goes to front of desk. Hand outstretched*) Let me explain it.

196

KELLERMAN

There's no need! P for Pal. Any Tec could get at the meaning o' this.... There's enough here to send us down for five years apiece.

CLITTERHOUSE
(*Coming forward*)
Give me back that book, Kellerman.

KELLERMAN
(*Crosses front of coffee table. Book under arm*)
Not bloody likely!

CLITTERHOUSE
You heard what I said? (*They face each other across table.*)

KELLERMAN
I shan't sleep until I've seen this burnt!

CLITTERHOUSE
Burnt....

KELLERMAN
You bet it'll be burnt.... D'you think I'm going to let you walk out on us—and keep this?

CLITTERHOUSE
Kellerman, give me back that book at once.

KELLERMAN
You try and get it!

CLITTERHOUSE
That book is very important, Kellerman. I'm not going to have my work destroyed by you!

KELLERMAN

It's a damn sight more important to me.... And you're not going to ditch us, anyway!

CLITTERHOUSE

Make yourself clear....

KELLERMAN

(*Pause. Changes book to under left arm*)

Have you ever thought what I could give the office about you?

CLITTERHOUSE

That's *not* very clear....

KELLERMAN

I've got myself covered, see? ... And they can't put anything on Daisy, because she's only did a bit of minding, now and again.

CLITTERHOUSE

Do you mean that you intend to give me away to the police?

KELLERMAN

It only wants one word.

CLITTERHOUSE

(*Pause*)

I see.... (*Turns. Crosses to desk. Sits on the edge of it.*)

KELLERMAN

You queered things for me with Daisy.... Now I can put them straight.... And I'll stop that sarcastic "Mister" Keller-man of yours, too!

CLITTERHOUSE

Will you, Mr. Kellerman!

KELLERMAN

That's all right, you come it while you can—but listen to this.... You've been picking the jobs—now I'll do the picking.

CLITTERHOUSE

Just what do you mean by that?

KELLERMAN

Well, I've got my eye on a bank....

CLITTERHOUSE

Are you suggesting that I should break into it?

KELLERMAN

I'm not suggesting. I'm telling you. (*Book across knee*) And I'll give you twenty per cent of what you take....

CLITTERHOUSE

(*Pause. Goes behind coffee table to mantelpiece*)

Rather harsh terms, Mr. Kellerman.... Does Oakie know you intend to suggest them?

KELLERMAN

No.... But if you try any funny business, I'll stop you, and they'll go along inside with you.

CLITTERHOUSE

(*Turns*)

I think I understand. Now you give me back that book?

KELLERMAN

Not on your life! ... And I haven't finished yet! It's just occurred to me I didn't make as much as I ought to have done out of those furs.

CLITTERHOUSE

Didn't you?

KELLERMAN

You wouldn't want to see me lose on the job, would you? ... Not if you could pass me back a thousand or so to put it right!

CLITTERHOUSE

You are making yourself quite clear—now.

KELLERMAN

I thought I was.... Awkward for you, isn't it?

CLITTERHOUSE

(*Turns away to lower end of fireplace*)

Yes, a little perhaps.... (*Pause*) Kellerman, do you realize the position into which you are trying to force me?

KELLERMAN

Trying! I know where I've got you! Now! Tomorrow night at the Club. We'll have a little talk about that bank job, and you can bring the thousand along with you. Not the flat, mind you. (*Angrily*) You keep away from Daisy, see! (CLITTERHOUSE *turns to mantelpiece, and sees tumbler.* KELLERMAN *pauses. Turns, still watching* CLITTERHOUSE *as he crosses and sits in chair.* CLITTERHOUSE *picks it up, and gradually the idea of drugging* KELLERMAN *comes to him.*)

KELLERMAN

Now, I'd like a little drink. (*Keeps book under arm.*)

CLITTERHOUSE

I was about to suggest one! (*Puts down tumbler.* CLITTER-
HOUSE *opens panel in front pedestal, extracting decanter, etc.,
and placing them on desk.*)

KELLERMAN

(*Looking through book*)

Nothing like a drink when you got something to think about,
is there?

CLITTERHOUSE

(*Standing across corner of desk, pouring drinks. His back
is to* KELLERMAN)

That's a remarkably apt observation, Mr. Kellerman.

KELLERMAN

Not that you've got any thinking to do. . . . I'll do that for
you.

CLITTERHOUSE

Kellerman, do you seriously mean all you've said?

KELLERMAN

(*Looks at him*)

You try and cross me!

CLITTERHOUSE

I only wanted to know. . . .

KELLERMAN

You behave sensible, and there won't be no hard feelings.

CLITTERHOUSE

Well, it seems better to be as friendly as possible ... for the time we'll be together. (*Turning, with* KELLERMAN'S *glass in his hand*) Soda?

KELLERMAN

Not for me.... (CLITTERHOUSE *splashes soda in own glass. Then turns with both. Hands glass to* KELLERMAN) Here's luck. (CLITTERHOUSE *watches* KELLERMAN *drain his glass. Then takes a sip of his own*) Now, I'll have another.... (*Gives glass to* CLITTERHOUSE) Soda this time.

CLITTERHOUSE

I get this sent down specially from Scotland.... How do you like it? (*He turns to desk again.*)

KELLERMAN

Oh! It's a bit ... I don't know. Got a full flavor.... It's all right, though. (CLITTERHOUSE *turns to him with bottle and glass in one hand, and syphon in other.*)

CLITTERHOUSE

That's very pleasing.... (*Hands glass. He pours soda into glass as* KELLERMAN *holds it.*)

KELLERMAN

Thanks.... You know you're going to get a lot more notes for that book of yours. (*Sitting with book on arm of chair and under his own forearm.*)

CLITTERHOUSE

You mean, while you blackmail me?

KELLERMAN

I wouldn't call it that, if I was you. . . .

CLITTERHOUSE

Oh, well, let it pass. (*Crosses to top of desk. Puts bottle and syphon down*) You are quite right about those notes, though.

KELLERMAN

But you don't get these. (*Tapping book.*)

CLITTERHOUSE

You think not? . . .

KELLERMAN

I'm sure not!

CLITTERHOUSE
(*Sits at desk chair*)

Anyway, I've just realized that my notes would hardly have been complete.

KELLERMAN

You're not likely to write that book now, are you?

CLITTERHOUSE

No? . . . (*Slowly*) You see I've collected a great deal of information about the various forms of criminal activity. But so far I have overlooked a major interest.

KELLERMAN

Oh, yes?

CLITTERHOUSE

I don't know anything whatever about the reactions associated with the greatest crime of all. . . .

KELLERMAN

What's that?

CLITTERHOUSE

Why ... disposing of someone.

KELLERMAN

You mean, doing somebody in?

CLITTERHOUSE

That would complete my book.

KELLERMAN

And it would complete you too! You can't get away with murder! (*Drinks.*)

CLITTERHOUSE

I rather think I could. You know a medical man has knowledge and opportunity denied to most people.

KELLERMAN

Don't you believe it! (**KELLERMAN** *settles in chair with head back and arms on arms of chair. Book still under forearm.*)

CLITTERHOUSE

But it's so simple. I've got it all worked out.

KELLERMAN

Have you? (*Without much interest, now that the heroin takes hold of him.*)

CLITTERHOUSE

I should make my victim unconscious, but I shouldn't actually end his life until I was quite ready to dispose of him.

KELLERMAN

Wouldn't you? (*His eyes are closed.*)

CLITTERHOUSE

No, that would be much too dangerous. . . . I should put him in the back of my car—under some rugs, perhaps. . . . Then I should drive down to Burnham-on-Crouch. . . . I have a little cottage there which backs on to the river. . . . I should put him in a punt. . . . Then I should go out to mid-stream, but I shouldn't drop him overboard until I was absolutely certain I had not been observed and that I was quite safe. Being unconscious, he would drown. . . . The coroner's verdict would be simply—found drowned. . . . There would be no marks . . . no violence . . . nothing.

KELLERMAN

Here—I feel sleepy! (*Suspicion in voice. But his speech is blurred and he makes very little movement. His eyes open and his fingers move a little.*)

CLITTERHOUSE

Of course you do, Mr. Kellerman. You're going to sleep.

KELLERMAN

Oh! No, I'm not! (*Feet move and fingers grip arms of chair, but no body movement.*)

CLITTERHOUSE

Oh, yes, you are. Do you remember that full taste in your whisky? I emptied a phial of heroin tablets into your first glass—twelve of them, a full grain. You see, you created an impossible situation, Mr. Kellerman. You forced me to do it. (KELLERMAN *pulls himself up a very little.*)

KELLERMAN

(*Speaking with effort*)
What the 'ell have you done to me?

CLITTERHOUSE

We're going to Burnham-on-Crouch! Mr. Kellerman! (KELLERMAN *slumps back into the chair, the manuscript book falling to the floor.*)

Curtain

ACT THREE

Scene II

Scene: *Same as Scene I. Forty-eight hours later.*

CLITTERHOUSE *is at his desk, writing.* NURSE ANN *enters, crosses to desk. She hands him two papers, but hides the third against her skirt.*

CLITTERHOUSE
Ah, thank you. (*The telephone bell rings*) See who it is, will you? (ANN *answers phone.*)

ANN
Hello . . . Oh, yes, Mr. Davidson?

CLITTERHOUSE
(*Looking up*)
In the morning!

ANN
I'm afraid it's hardly possible for you to see the doctor this evening, unless it is very urgent. (CLITTERHOUSE *puts one paper down and takes another*) Oh, most certainly in the morning. . . . Yes, at a quarter to ten. . . . Take just one—the last thing tonight. . . . In the morning, then. . . . Good-bye, Mr. Davidson. (ANN *replaces receiver.*)

CLITTERHOUSE
(*Throwing second paper aside*)
There's really nothing the matter with him . . . he worries . . . where's the evening news?

ANN

Here, Doctor.... (*She slowly produces it*) There's a photograph in it.... (*She holds Clitterhouse with her gaze as she hands him the paper. He still looks at her after he has taken it. His glance goes to the photograph*) Isn't that the man who called himself Mr. Benjamin?

CLITTERHOUSE

(*Looks at her and then back at paper*)

Yes....

ANN

The paper calls him Benny Kellerman.... Isn't he the fence you once said you were going to see?

CLITTERHOUSE

Ah, you remember.... (*He is looking at paper "without seeing it."*)

ANN

Doctor, I saw him here—two evenings ago.

CLITTERHOUSE

Yes! That's right, Nurse.... (*Props paper up on phone.*)

ANN

He's been missing since he came here!

CLITTERHOUSE

Yes, he has ... hasn't he?

ANN

Something has happened—I know it!

CLITTERHOUSE

Something certainly seems to have happened to Mr. Kellerman.

ANN

He was not... found drowned!

CLITTERHOUSE
(*Sharply looking up*)

He was!

ANN

Read what it says there.... The police are investigating!
(HE *unfolds paper and reads for first time*) Says he was dead
before he went into the River Crouch! (*Slight pause*) A grain
of heroin must have been too much for him....

CLITTERHOUSE
(*Turns to her*)

What d'you mean by that?

ANN
(*Speaks slowly*)

When I came back from Nurse Harvey's, that phial on your
desk was empty. You'd gone out. You didn't come back till
after two o'clock in the morning—I waited for you—I knew
that something was wrong.

CLITTERHOUSE

Nurse, aren't you letting your imagination get the better
of you?

ANN

I don't think I am.... Did you take him to Burnham?

CLITTERHOUSE
(*Rises, facing her*)
Nurse, you don't realize what you're saying!

ANN
Do you realize that they'll trace him to you?

CLITTERHOUSE
They cannot possibly do that!

ANN
Did you ... kill him?

CLITTERHOUSE
(*Turns a step toward her*)
Nurse, I don't want ...

ANN
(*Quickly*)
Did you? ...

CLITTERHOUSE
(*Slowly. Turns*)
Yes, I did. . . . I had to. . . . He was blackmailing me. Forcing me to go on.

ANN
(*Whispering*)
Oh, my God . . .

CLITTERHOUSE
Everything all right. . . . Then, suddenly, it all got out of hand!

ANN

I can't believe it.... (*Moves to behind chair.*)

CLITTERHOUSE

It seems scarcely possible to me. (*Coming back to desk.*)

ANN

Then you did give him that heroin?

CLITTERHOUSE

Yes....

ANN

(*Turns*)

They'll find it.... It must have been too much for his heart....

CLITTERHOUSE

I examined him before I took him on the river. He was alive then.

ANN

You meant him to drown but he must have died on the boat.

CLITTERHOUSE

I didn't examine him again....

ANN

Why didn't you stop before this? Oh, that book—that damned book!

CLITTERHOUSE

(*Turns, moves to desk*)

You're getting hysterical, Nurse!

211

ANN

You must destroy that book! If there's the least suspicion, it will give you away!

CLITTERHOUSE

They can't possibly trace anything to me. (*Moves up behind chair.*)

ANN

How do you know? ... You have made one slip already!

CLITTERHOUSE

Yes. ... He was not "found drowned."

ANN

Going to Burnham—that was another!

CLITTERHOUSE

I don't think it was.

ANN

You may have made a third!

CLITTERHOUSE

No! You know, Nurse. ... We're frightening each other, aren't we? ... Listen, there is absolutely nothing that can link Kellerman with me.

ANN

Then why did he come here? You didn't tell him who you were, surely?

CLITTERHOUSE

No, I don't know how he found that out.

ANN

Suppose someone else knows!

CLITTERHOUSE

Nobody else knows—he said so!

ANN

That may have been a lie!

CLITTERHOUSE

I don't think it was....

ANN

But you haven't questioned it until now, have you? You haven't been thinking clearly, Doctor. You were not *able* to think. Oh, why did I obey you at the beginning? Why didn't I get Hillery?

CLITTERHOUSE

Don't be absurd!

ANN

(Turns)

You'd been overworking . . . you were overwrought . . . I realize it now.

CLITTERHOUSE

Nurse.... Please!

ANN

You were just like a patient who won't give in ... forcing a new interest to keep yourself going.

CLITTERHOUSE

You are talking nonsense. Good Lord, I'm just the same as I have always been. (*Sits at desk.*)

ANN

I could have stopped all this.... Oh, I'm so frightened for you ... so frightened! (*The telephone bell rings.* ANN *moves to telephone.*)

CLITTERHOUSE

No. Let me.... You calm down, Nurse.... (*Lifts receiver*) Hello.... Yes, it is.... What? The police? (ANN *turns, looks at* CLITTERHOUSE) Well, this is Doctor Clitterhouse speaking ... Clitterhouse.... Oh, you only have the number.... Look here, I don't understand this. You'll find my address in the telephone book! ... In that case, I suggest you should get into touch with Inspector Charles at the Yard.... He knows me quite well.... Oh, no, but it is a little disconcerting to be ... very well. Good-bye. (*Replaces receiver.*)

ANN

The police! What did they want?

CLITTERHOUSE

(*Slowly looking out*)

Apparently, they had a telephone number and wanted to know whose it was. So they simply rang up.

ANN

Why?

CLITTERHOUSE

(*Not looking at her*)

The man said they were making some inquiries.

214

ANN

About . . . Kellerman?

CLITTERHOUSE

Of course not! He didn't say what it was about.

ANN

I don't like it!

CLITTERHOUSE
(*Rises*)

Just because they happened to have my telephone number, it doesn't mean that they connect me with anything.

ANN
(*Turns*)

But they must have been in a hurry. . . . Why didn't they go to the telephone authorities to find out?

CLITTERHOUSE

It may have been the wrong number, anyhow! (*Telephone bell rings again. ANN moves to answer it*) Let me, they may be calling again. (*Lifts receiver*) Hello? This sounds like a call-box. . . . Oakie? . . . How the devil did you get this number? . . . Kellerman what? And they found it in his pocket? Listen, don't stop for anything. Get away now, and look after Daisy. Don't stay talking to me. Get away now. Good luck . . . and to Pal. Good luck. . . . Good-bye! (*Replaces receiver.*)

ANN

Who was that?

CLITTERHOUSE

They've been to Kellerman's club . . . making inquiries.

215

ANN

They've found out?

CLITTERHOUSE

Apparently. I'd used a telephone, and he'd fitted something to it that registered my number, and they found it in his pocket.... That's why the police telephoned me!

ANN

In his pocket!

CLITTERHOUSE

I didn't search him.... I shouldn't have known what the thing was, anyway....

ANN

That's the ... third slip!

CLITTERHOUSE
(*Sits in fireside chair*)
If they're quick, they can all get away ... just in case. (*Speaking almost to himself.*)

ANN

Doctor, you must get away, too!

CLITTERHOUSE

No.... Oh, no!

ANN

Can't you see the mistakes you've made! First going to Burnham at all ... then the heroin was too much ... now the telephone! Why, it's like a net ... closing round you!

216

CLITTERHOUSE

There's an opening to every net.... There has to be.

ANN

They'll come here.... That book will give you away....
(*Crosses quickly to desk*) You must get rid of it!

CLITTERHOUSE

No.... No! ... (*She stops near chair*) That's too valuable
to lose, whatever happens.

ANN
(*Turns*)

Please ... please be guided by me.... I'll deny that he ever
came here ... I'll account for all the heroin!

CLITTERHOUSE

No! That wouldn't be any use....

ANN

When they come, I'll say that I slipped over to Nurse
Harvey and you were still here when I came back ... working, Doctor, we were doing accounts—anything!

CLITTERHOUSE
(*Rises, crosses to her*)

No, no! ... I won't involve you. Now—wait! (*Pause*) You
can't dodge the police.... They ask endless questions. They
keep probing.... They would break down any alibi.

ANN

Oh, no. They wouldn't break me down, Doctor!

217

CLITTERHOUSE

They might simply not believe you.... Anyway, that's no use. There's . . . (*Breaks off. Pause. Goes to desk chair. Sits*) Nurse ... I said there was an opening to every net! (*He lifts the telephone receiver. Looks at telephone pad for number and dials quickly.*)

ANN

What are you going to do?

CLITTERHOUSE
(*Dialing*)

Kellerman was a worthless type ... a blackmailer.... He forced my hand.... There are extenuating circumstances! We'll see what ... (*To telephone*) Oh! Is Sir William at home? ... Could I have a word with him? This is Doctor Clitterhouse speaking.... Thank you.

ANN

You're going to talk to Sir William about it?

CLITTERHOUSE

I'm going to take counsel's opinion.

ANN

Oh, Doctor. He can have only one opinion!

CLITTERHOUSE

He told me the other day that he could always make a diagnosis from facts. I'll give him the facts now. When I ... ah! (*In phone*) Sir William? This is Clitterhouse speaking. How are you? That's excellent! Sir William, there's a rather urgent matter that I should like to discuss with you. Could I slip over to see you right away? Oh, you're leaving the house now? Well, if you would drop in, it's only just across the road. Oh, thank you, Sir William. Good-bye. (*Replaces phone.*)

ANN

Do be careful what you say....

CLITTERHOUSE

I can talk to him in confidence.

ANN

But what can you hope to gain?

CLITTERHOUSE

His opinion.... He says that given the facts he can always assess the outcome of a case.... He knew that he would get Maynard off.... And this book may help.

ANN

Oh, no. It will go against you!

CLITTERHOUSE

I don't think it will.

ANN

I'd rather see it destroyed.

CLITTERHOUSE

No.... This must not be destroyed whatever happens.

ANN

Think of yourself ... not the book.

CLITTERHOUSE

The book's more important than I am.... Nurse, you will help me with this, won't you?

ANN

Yes. I'll do anything . . . anything!

CLITTERHOUSE

You could have the manuscript prepared for me.... There are heaps of things that you could do. (*The bell rings*) That'll be Sir William! (ANN *hurries out.* CLITTERHOUSE *collects the newspapers from the desk and puts them under cushion at head of couch. Then goes toward the door as* ANN *re-enters, holding door open.*)

ANN

Sir William Grant. (SIR WILLIAM *enters. They shake hands.*)

CLITTERHOUSE

Good evening, Sir William.

SIR WILLIAM

Good evening!

CLITTERHOUSE

You're looking better. (ANN *exits.*)

SIR WILLIAM

I feel it.... Went round in seventy-six today. I astounded myself!

CLITTERHOUSE

Back to your old form, eh?

220

SIR WILLIAM

I was lucky from the start. I happened to get away with a screaming drive. You know the Fold course, don't you?

CLITTERHOUSE

Yes! I've often played there....

SIR WILLIAM

I passed that double bunker ... three hundred yards if it's an inch!

CLITTERHOUSE

Good shot!

SIR WILLIAM

I found the ball in a fair sort of lie. Not quite good enough for a brassie, and not bad enough for an iron. So I used my spoon and ... Well, I was on! (CLITTERHOUSE *glances nervously at clock during this speech.*)

CLITTERHOUSE

On in two?

SIR WILLIAM

On in two and about seventeen feet from the pin! ... And I sunk it!

CLITTERHOUSE

That hole's a bogie five!

SIR WILLIAM

Of course it is.... That gave me an eagle ... my first in five years, Clitterhouse.... Congratulate me!

CLITTERHOUSE

What a day!

SIR WILLIAM

An eagle on the first! ... Lord love me, Clitterhouse, it was worth living for!

CLITTERHOUSE

After that you couldn't do wrong!

SIR WILLIAM

The finest round I can remember! I'm not one of your tigers, you know.

CLITTERHOUSE

I'm afraid my best up there is eighty-six....

SIR WILLIAM

We must have a round together some time. Can you get away tomorrow?

CLITTERHOUSE

I'm afraid tomorrow seems a little doubtful, Sir William.

SIR WILLIAM

I suppose so. (*Rises*) You fellows never know what's going to crop up, do you? However, bear it in mind.

CLITTERHOUSE

Oh! I shall.... I do hope we get a game together—soon.

SIR WILLIAM

Yes! Well, I didn't come over to talk golf, did I? There was something you wanted, wasn't there?

CLITTERHOUSE

Yes! (*Pause*) I'm afraid it will be rather talking shop from your point of view, Sir William.

SIR WILLIAM

(*Sits back and crosses legs*)

Oh, well. Go ahead! Pick my brains as much as you like.... I'm in a good mood!

CLITTERHOUSE

Well, it's like this.... A very close friend of mine seems to have gone off the rails.

SIR WILLIAM

Oh? ... Professionally?

CLITTERHOUSE

I'll explain.... (*Sits in desk chair*) He had the idea of trying to secure data on the nervous reactions of—well, crooks.

SIR WILLIAM

Oh.... Yes?

CLITTERHOUSE

He felt that their experiences must have a definite influence, not only upon their psychology, but upon their physique.

SIR WILLIAM

I think I follow you.

CLITTERHOUSE

(*Leans eagerly across desk*)

He wanted, amongst other things, to discover the medical

223

reasons for these influences. By tests and close observation, whilst the crooks were actually at work.

SIR WILLIAM

Yes! Yes.... There might be something in it.

CLITTERHOUSE

He found that there was!

SIR WILLIAM

Oh! Er— He's been carrying out this investigation?

CLITTERHOUSE

Yes....

SIR WILLIAM
(Uncrosses legs. With more interest)

Did you say ... while the crooks were actually at work?

CLITTERHOUSE

I did.

SIR WILLIAM

Oh.... How did he manage that?

CLITTERHOUSE

He simply ... went amongst crooks.

SIR WILLIAM

Fraternized with them?

CLITTERHOUSE

Rather more.... He actually joined them.

224

SIR WILLIAM

Good heavens! ... (*Rises. Takes off coat and puts it on fire-side chair*) Are you ... are you suggesting that he ... well, that he resorted to criminal practices?

CLITTERHOUSE

He had to—to find out what he wanted.

SIR WILLIAM

Oh, did he? (*Goes to mantelpiece between chair and coffee table.*)

CLITTERHOUSE

He worked alone at first—on quite small burglaries.... Then he met a receiver, and other men and, between them, they did some quite reasonably clever jobs.

SIR WILLIAM

And he's involved himself, I suppose? (*Strikes match from mantel and lights cigar.*)

CLITTERHOUSE

He has.... Some of the robberies were what the newspapers called sensational.

SIR WILLIAM

And your medical friend was in them?

CLITTERHOUSE

Yes, collecting data....

SIR WILLIAM

Yes, but did I understand you to say that he jeopardized his practice to do this?

CLITTERHOUSE

Yes.

SIR WILLIAM

Well, what happened to the proceeds of these robberies?

CLITTERHOUSE

The crooks had their share, and he gave his away anony-
mously. . . . His object was research, you see.

SIR WILLIAM

Well, I don't know that I do see, quite. . . . I suppose it has
got rather beyond him, is that it?

CLITTERHOUSE

Yes. . . . He kept his identity secret. . . . Then one of the
crooks discovered who he was and tried to blackmail him.

SIR WILLIAM

That was inevitable.

CLITTERHOUSE

That man was a fence.

SIR WILLIAM

I know the kind.

CLITTERHOUSE

My friend's notes were then practically complete. He didn't
want to go on. Only this man tried to force him to continue.

SIR WILLIAM

And then?

226

CLITTERHOUSE
(*Almost to himself*)

He suddenly realized that he'd studied various types of criminal activity, from burglary to, well, organized robbery, but so far he lacked any data on the—ultimate crime.

SIR WILLIAM
(*Pause*)

Not murder?

CLITTERHOUSE

Yes....

SIR WILLIAM
(*Pause*)

And he has? ...

CLITTERHOUSE
(*Pause*)

He has. ...

SIR WILLIAM

You mean ... removed ... the blackmailer!

CLITTERHOUSE

Yes....

SIR WILLIAM

He would, of course....

CLITTERHOUSE

Why do you say that?

SIR WILLIAM

Never mind . . . go on.

CLITTERHOUSE

There isn't any more. . . .

SIR WILLIAM

Except that he has his last chapter.

CLITTERHOUSE

In every detail. . . .

SIR WILLIAM

And he is now afraid that the police will be after him?

CLITTERHOUSE

Well, he does appreciate that contingency. Yes, Sir William. . . .

SIR WILLIAM

(Short pause)

They will, you know!

CLITTERHOUSE

Why do you say that?

SIR WILLIAM

Because that kind of man would make mistakes—fatal errors. He'd miss things.

CLITTERHOUSE

How can you be so sure of that?

228

SIR WILLIAM

Because his every thought and action was focused on an end—and not the means to it.

CLITTERHOUSE

Oh....

SIR WILLIAM

He was intent only on his idea. So obsessed that he could commit—*murder*.

CLITTERHOUSE

But his hand *was* rather forced.

SIR WILLIAM

But he might have met the man's demands in a way other than by killing him.

CLITTERHOUSE

He couldn't see any other way.

SIR WILLIAM

Naturally, he couldn't.... He was obsessed by his objective.

CLITTERHOUSE

Oh....

SIR WILLIAM

Tell me, Clitterhouse, are you stating a hypothetical case—or has this actually happened?

CLITTERHOUSE

Well, let's assume that it has actually happened.

229

SIR WILLIAM

Well, what then?

CLITTERHOUSE

What would be my friend's chances of getting off?

SIR WILLIAM

It isn't a matter of chances at all.

CLITTERHOUSE

Isn't it?

SIR WILLIAM

He would get off!

CLITTERHOUSE

What! ... Why?

SIR WILLIAM

Because the man's as mad as a hatter!

CLITTERHOUSE
(*Leans back*)

Good ... Lord!

SIR WILLIAM

It's obvious. ...

CLITTERHOUSE

And ... he'd get off?

SIR WILLIAM

The facts being as stated by you, I would stake my reputation on it!

230

CLITTERHOUSE

Stake your reputation. . . . Well, I'll be damned!

SIR WILLIAM

It would not be worth bringing him to trial. . . .

CLITTERHOUSE

But the man's not mad, Sir William!

SIR WILLIAM

Well, he may not go about with straws in his hair, but he isn't sane, and therefore he isn't responsible.

CLITTERHOUSE

But—er—what about his book?

SIR WILLIAM

Well, that might be quite coherent and perfectly sane and sensible. He probably goes about and acts just like anybody else.

CLITTERHOUSE

Just like you and me?

SIR WILLIAM

Yes. And you'll have to do something about it, you know.

CLITTERHOUSE

What do you mean?

SIR WILLIAM

Well, you're an accessory after the fact! I take it that you have come by this information confidentially—but you can't keep it to yourself.

231

CLITTERHOUSE

Oh. . . .

SIR WILLIAM

Your friend must be restrained. . . . I suggest that you ought, immediately, to inform the proper authorities. (*The bell rings in the hall.*)

CLITTERHOUSE
(*Looks toward door*)

The proper authorities!

SIR WILLIAM
(*Rises, crosses to above desk*)

Of course, I don't want to propose any breach of confidence but . . . does it happen to be anybody whom I know?

CLITTERHOUSE

Yes. . . . You do know him, Sir William.

SIR WILLIAM

Indeed? . . . Who? . . .

CLITTERHOUSE
(*Pointing at himself*)

Me. . . .

SIR WILLIAM

Good God. . . . (*The door opens.* NURSE ANN *and then* INSPECTOR CHARLES *enter, followed by* SERGEANT BATES.)

CLITTERHOUSE
(*Quietly*)

Hello, Charley. . . . (SIR WILLIAM *turns on hearing door open.* ANN *stands near door.*)

232

CHARLES
(*Quietly*)
Hello, old man.... Good evening, Sir William.

SIR WILLIAM
Good evening, Charles. (CHARLES *turns, nods to* SERGEANT, *who comes forward, hat in hand, in front of* SIR WILLIAM. *Faces* CLITTERHOUSE.)

SERGEANT
(*To* SIR WILLIAM)
Excuse me, sir.... (*Looks closely at* CLITTERHOUSE) Yes, sir.... This is the man I saw in Kellerman's club about four months ago.

CLITTERHOUSE
(*Quietly*)
Ah, you remember me?

SERGEANT
(*Emphatically*)
I do!

SIR WILLIAM
What is this, Charles?

CHARLES
Clit, I wonder if you'd come down to the Yard with me ... if you're not too busy?

CLITTERHOUSE
Why, of course, Charley.... We promised ourselves an evening out, didn't we?

233

CHARLES

What have you been up to, old man?

SIR WILLIAM

(*Steps in. Touches him on shoulder*)

Doctor! ... I don't think I'd say ... very much.

CHARLES

(*To* SERGEANT BATES)

All right, Sergeant. You can wait in the hall.

SERGEANT

Very good, sir.... (*He exits.* CHARLES *watches him off,'then turns.*)

CHARLES

(*Faces* CLITTERHOUSE)

You know why I'm here, old man, don't you?

CLITTERHOUSE

Yes, I know....

CHARLES

Benny Kellerman....

SIR WILLIAM

Was that the man, Clitterhouse?

CLITTERHOUSE

Yes....

SIR WILLIAM

Is this an arrest, Charles?

234

CHARLES

No.... (*Bows his head*) I couldn't do that.... We just want to ask you a few questions.

CLITTERHOUSE

Well, don't be so upset about it, Charley.... Everything's all right, isn't it, Sir William?

SIR WILLIAM

Why, yes, of course.

CLITTERHOUSE

(*Reaching for manuscript book*)
Sir William, would you mind taking charge of this for me?

SIR WILLIAM

What is it? (SIR WILLIAM *takes it.*)

CLITTERHOUSE

My medical notes.... Nurse!

ANN

Yes, Doctor....

CLITTERHOUSE

You won't forget that you promised to help with that?

ANN

I'll do anything that I can....

CLITTERHOUSE

Charley, did you see Daisy?

235

CHARLES

Yes, for a few moments.

CLITTERHOUSE

She's not in this, you know.

CHARLES

No, they allowed her to go. . . . Clit, what is all this about?

CLITTERHOUSE

Well, I thought it was because he was trying to black-mail me.

CHARLES
(*Quickly*)

And was he?

CLITTERHOUSE

I'm not so sure now. . . . I think he was helping me to write a book. (SIR WILLIAM *makes a slight sign to* CHARLES.)

CHARLES

I see, Sir William.

CLITTERHOUSE

Yes. Sir William will insist that I'm . . .

CHARLES
(*Breaks in*)

Will you come along now, old man? (*Goes to door, opens it.*)

CLITTERHOUSE

Of course. Nurse.

236

ANN

Yes, Doctor?

CLITTERHOUSE

You don't think I'm ... (*Bows his head*) Do you?

ANN

No! Of course not, Doctor.

CLITTERHOUSE

Be honest.

ANN

You've been overworking, that's all.... You'll be all right in a little while.

CLITTERHOUSE
(*Turns. Holds* ANN's *hand*)

Sir William, may I retain you to represent me?

SIR WILLIAM
(*Steps down*)

Why, naturally, my friend.

CLITTERHOUSE
(*Taking both her hands*)

Ann, you've been a brick.... When I come back I'll buy you a little woolly dog.... Does that sound crazy? .... Work it out! ... Come along, Charley. (*He goes to door.* ANN *goes quickly to chair, then stops and turns, looking at* CLITTER-HOUSE. *He turns at door*) Sir William!

237

SIR WILLIAM

Yes?

CLITTERHOUSE

You won't forget, will you, Sir William—your reputation is at stake? I shall be very upset if you lose it. (*He exits, followed by* CHARLES.)

Curtain